BLOCKING THE NOISE

DR. ANGELINA LIPMAN

BLOCKING THE NOISE

A Roadmap to Happiness

DR. ANGELINA LIPMAN

Copyright © 2025 by Dr. Angelina Lipman.
All rights reserved.

Published in the United States.

Library of Congress Cataloging-in-Publication Data
is available upon request.

Hardcover ISBN: 979-8-9908089-1-1

Paperback ISBN 979-8-9908089-0-4

eBook ISBN 979-8-9908089-2-8

Audiobook ISBN 979-8-9908089-1-1

Printed in the United States.

Book design: Casalino Design

Copy editing: Will Palmer

Proofreading: Mary White

Illustrations © Adobestock and Casalino Design

10 9 8 7 6 5 4 3 2 1

First Edition

DEDICATION:

To Monte, Remy, Juliet, and Cameron, thank you for your love, support, and guidance on this journey to blocking the noise.

CONTENTS

INTRODUCTION — 9

CHAPTER 1
MEET NOISE — 19

CHAPTER 2
PLAYING OUR ROLES — 33

CHAPTER 3
SAFEGUARDING HAPPINESS — 45

CHAPTER 4
MASTERING THE ART
OF ACCEPTANCE — 55

CHAPTER 5
FORGIVENESS
AND LETTING GO — 67

CHAPTER 6
ASSEMBLING YOUR A-TEAM — 73

**CHAPTER 7
INTRODUCING YOURSELF
TO . . . YOURSELF**   83

**CHAPTER 8
IDENTIFYING NOISY THOUGHTS**   97

**CHAPTER 9
BECOMING FEARLESS**   113

**CHAPTER 10
BLOCKING THE NOISE FOR GOOD**   129

**APPENDIX
BLOCKING THE NOISE:
QUICK TIPS AND CHEAT SHEETS**   143

ABOUT THE AUTHOR   146

ACKNOWLEDGMENTS   147

JOURNAL PAGES   149

INTRODUCTION

"Angelina, you're going to be a mother."

It was the most wonderful—and terrifying—news I'd ever received. As the doctor rattled on about symptoms, diets, and due dates, my thoughts ping-ponged between confident and clueless, from "I can't wait to tell my family" to "How do you spell 'epidural'?"

A research psychologist by trade, I left the doctor's office with every pamphlet available—this was back in the olden days, before smartphones—and made a beeline for the nearest bookstore, where I stocked up on all the latest and greatest books for expecting parents. What I soon came to realize was that motherhood was going to be the greatest experience of my life—and, potentially, the noisiest.

Motherhood is noisy. I don't just mean the bleeps and bloops of video games, wails so loud they'll haunt your dreams, or the buzz of preteens raiding the fridge in between adventures. As a mother to three amazing kids, I do know how constant (not to mention annoying) the sounds of childhood can be. But the noise I'm talking about is a bit more insidious. It's sneaky, deceptive, and, though no one can hear it but you, louder than the Xbox game echoing from your living room.

Noise is the pressure we put on ourselves to finish our to-do lists, in between Jenny's dental appointment at 2 and Junior's softball game at 5. It's juggling a household and a job along with all of our relationships; it's the murmur of our never-ending daily responsibilities. It's the uncertainty of raising kids in a world we hardly recognize, and the devastating push notifications alerting us to yet another tragedy that steals our breath and stops our heart.

Noise is every anxiety we have as we struggle to make the right decision for our families. It's the fear of what might happen if we buck tradition, defy convention, or follow our own intuition about mothering. Every unexamined child-rearing tip inherited from your parents' generation, every expectation you unknowingly have about your child, every sinking feeling that no one besides you seems to be questioning their legitimacy as a mother—all of it is noise.

Sometimes the noise is deafening; other times it's a low hush. But whatever its volume, it's my belief that noise is the sum of what stands between us and happiness.

MY STORY

Before I was a mom, I was a research psychologist.

It wasn't my initial plan. When I started my freshman year at Columbia University, I thought I'd become a newscaster. I wish I could say I had a lifelong passion for the incredible impact of award-winning journalism, but alas, it wasn't that deep. People always told me I had a calming voice—as a kid I was always chosen to read *The Night Before Christmas* aloud at school when the holidays rolled around—and I thought maybe I could make a career out of it.

All of that changed when I took my first psychology course. Right away, it was my *thing*. I think I even read the course textbook from cover to cover in one night. The study of human behavior was fascinating to me. I enjoyed every aspect of the field, from the analytical to the behavioral to the anecdotal. Discovering, researching, and assessing a psychological dynamic was like putting together a complicated puzzle: difficult and challenging at first, but suddenly obvious and rewarding by the end.

I declared myself a psych major and things snowballed from there. One master's and a dual PhD later, I had a few successful publications under my belt and even found a niche that spoke to my heart: identity and the unconscious mind.

A TALE OF TWO MINDS

Most of us are familiar with the conscious mind: it's the part of us that uses logic and reason to make sense of our actions, behaviors, and beliefs, and it generally contains everything that we're aware of—both about ourselves and the world.

By contrast, the unconscious mind contains all that we're unaware of: what we once knew but forgot, what we're too ashamed to shine a light on, and how we react before we have a chance to respond. It's the source of our knee-jerk reactions and our inexplicable sore spots, of all the things we feel but can't rationally explain.

Simply put, the conscious mind is home to the urges, feelings, memories, thoughts, behaviors, beliefs, and desires that we know we have, while the unconscious mind is home to the urges, feelings, memories, thoughts, behaviors, beliefs, and desires that we're unaware of—the things we don't know about ourselves.

As I mentioned, much of my research was concerned with how our unconscious thoughts and beliefs interact with our various identities. In my research, I found that people who could connect with one aspect of their identity (say, an academic) without compromising another (like their gender or ethnicity) not only were more successful than those with less integrated identities, but they were also happier. Meanwhile, those who felt their self-expression was determined by—and often constrained by—their context or setting were more likely to suffer from anxiety, depression, and alienation than their peers.

It seemed to me that the key to happiness was the ability to inhabit multiple identities at once without inner conflict—to show up as your whole self. Of course, that's easier said than done. I'm sure you can think of a few times when one aspect of your identity clashed with another; it may even be all you know. As a Black woman from the world of academia, I certainly know how it feels to believe you must sacrifice aspects of yourself to succeed, or even just blend in. *If I just neutralize all the things that make me stand out*, the thought goes, *maybe I'll finally belong*.

My research highlighted what we all know deep down: happiness is the result of loving your whole self, accepting every part of who you are. So, if we all know this, why do we continue to reject aspects of ourselves?

One reason we fragment our identities is to protect them from hostility—to keep them safe from judgment, disrespect, or stereotyping. If we don't talk about motherhood at the workplace, for example, we don't have to worry about that part of our identities coming under attack. We can focus on what we came to do and be successful.

But what if that strategy—and the underlying noise that birthed it—actually makes us less successful, less happy? Can we accept that dividing ourselves up into digestible portions might actually be holding us back?

What I was learning about the unconscious mind and its impact on our psychological well-being was fascinating. It seemed to me that, more often than not, the problems we think we have are nothing compared with the stories we tell ourselves about those problems. If we keep replaying the story that we're inferior, incapable, unworthy, and unlovable—if we drown ourselves in noise—no amount of external validation or success will make us happy.

MOM VILLAGE

What I was discovering through my research had the power to change lives. I knew I needed to find a way to break these ideas out of the lab and into everyday life, where they could really make an impact. So, pregnant with my second child, I decided to become a stay-at-home mom and figure out my next move.

In hindsight, I'd probably made the choice to leave academia the first time I held my eldest son in my arms; it just took a while for my mind to catch up with my heart. Because, as much as I relished being a mom, I was conflicted about walking away from my life's work. Raised by a single mother with a demanding career, I felt beyond lucky to have the choice to walk away at all. But I'd also been an academic my entire adult life. It was part of my identity. Now, whenever someone asked me what I do—that inescapable ice-breaking question—I couldn't help but judge myself for my answer: I was just a mom.

Based on my own research, I knew that perceiving myself as "just a mom" was a recipe for unhappiness. It was noise, plain and simple. After all, I had never been just an academic, and I would never be just a mom, either. I was—I *am*—so much more than my roles. All of us are. At the same time, I had never learned to see myself outside of the context of the various roles I play. Who was I without them? I knew that if I could discover that, I would find true happiness.

Using everything I'd learned during my time in academia, I began to craft a process to "block the noise." I wanted to design a program that would help people—myself included—get back in touch with our whole selves. Selves that don't depend on our roles or achievements for our happiness, selves that live in recognition and appreciation of everything that makes us who we are, selves that can celebrate the people who shaped us and continue to influence us, the experiences we have had and will have, what we have learned and will learn, and how we see the world and those around us. The result is the book in your hands.

Why so much talk about moms? Well, for one thing, moms are my people. It was my own struggle to integrate the role of motherhood with my other identities that inspired me to create this process, and I want to honor that by paying it forward. Mothers are the most incredible group I've had the privilege of belonging to.

I also know how noisy motherhood can be. There's no shortage of ways to feel like you're falling short. Because even if we try to deny it, many of us still feel some mix of pressure and desire to be the Best . . . Mom . . . *Ever*! And instead of realizing that such lofty expectations are a recipe for disaster, we quietly forgo parts of our identity until all that's left is "Mom."

Suppressing our own needs and desires becomes instinctual, and when we do finally manage to put ourselves first, we feel guilty about it!

But what I've learned, from both my research and my experience, is that our happiness is the best gift we can give our children. (Okay, that and the latest iPhone.) The sad truth is that our bad moods, negative self-talk, resentment, and self-neglect—our noise—don't go unnoticed by our kids.

Kids are observant, and they're constantly picking up what we're putting down, whether we realize it or not.

But when we're genuinely happy, our kids feel it, too. By discovering what gives us joy and modeling the process for our children, we give them the tools they need to embark on their own unique journeys. When we hold space for our dreams and desires, we teach our kids how to hold space for theirs. Always remember that taking time to find your own happiness isn't selfish or neglectful; it's a priceless gift to your loved ones.

I think we all know that, intuitively, but it's so hard to break the spell and remember how to listen to ourselves again. That's what's at the core of this process: turning down the noise so that we can hear our true selves. Because at the end of the day, the journey to your happiness is one only you have the map for. No therapist, life coach, or guru can tell you what makes you happy—and neither can I. I'm here, in the form of this book, to guide you as you rediscover who you really are underneath all the noise.

> **BLOCKING THE NOISE IS FOR EVERYONE (NOT JUST MOMS)!** *The "motherhood" references throughout the book are a reflection of my own pathway to blocking the noise and achieving unwavering happiness. Within every chapter you will discover examples, constructs, tools, and exercises that act as stepping stones to self discovery and blocking YOUR noise. This book is a roadmap to personalized happiness accentuating, supporting, and enriching each person's unique journey.*

YOUR JOURNEY STARTS HERE

The process I outline in the following pages will reveal you . . . to yourself. Soon you'll discover that you're already the person most qualified to discover and nurture your own happiness—and you always have been. It will help you take inventory of everything you are and discover everything you want to be—and everything you didn't realize you *could* be.

As you read, you'll find opportunities and exercises to reflect, resolve, and redefine each chapter of your story. You'll start by witnessing and analyzing your relationships. Next, you'll move on to self-reflection and discovery. Finally, you'll learn how to live a fearless life that creates joy and fulfillment for yourself and everyone you love.

To help bring these concepts to life, I'll share some of my own experiences as a mother, with my family making a cameo here and there. The remaining stories and challenges I outline in this book are real, but the folks who experienced them are not: they're composite characters who exist solely to illustrate for you how noise functions in our lives. In other words, no relationships were harmed in the writing of this book, and any similarities to real people are coincidental.

I'm so excited to welcome you to this journey. While I can't promise that it'll be easy, I know firsthand that it's worth it. This process has reframed how I view my existence and the world around me. It enabled me to be unapologetically myself while gaining fresh perspective on, and appreciation for, the people in my life. In short, it helped me achieve happiness.

How will you know when you've achieved your happiness? It will wake you up every day, greet you throughout every step of your journey, sustain you in times of difficulty, and act as a lighthouse for others.

Until then, be gentle with yourself and enjoy the journey. Now, let's take the first step . . .

—*Dr. Angelina*

TOP 10 SOURCES

1. Your kids. From the tiniest boo-boo to the first big heartbreak, becoming a mom means sweating the small and large stuff, forever and ever, amen.

2. Your partner. You hail from a free-range household; they take after their helicopter parents. They want to stay at home with the kids and . . . so do you. Co-creating a family with your partner will take some negotiation . . . and a deep breath or two.

3. Your parents. Who knows more about parenting than your own parents? I mean, look at the amazing job they did with you!

4. Money. How to afford swim lessons, soccer uniforms, and the season's must-have sneakers (which your kid is guaranteed to outgrow by next season)? You don't know, but everyone sure expects you to!

5. Your extended family. Are your kids perfect angels who send prompt thank-you notes and babysit their cousins for free, or do they give Dennis the Menace a run for his money? Someone in your extended family will be sure to let you know!

OF MOM NOISE

6. Your pets. As you bend over to pick up Sparky's mess for the second time today—and the twelfth time this week—you seem to recall how his adoption was supposed to teach somebody about routine and responsibility . . . and you're pretty sure it wasn't you.

7. Your friends. Ah, the refuge of a relationship with an adult you're not related to! If only you could find the time to . . . do whatever it is you used to enjoy doing with them, when you had the time to do it.

8. Your job. Even if you once multitasked with the best of 'em, juggling kids and a job often means making a mountain of sacrifice for a sprinkle of recognition.

9. Your health. With all that you're just managing to manage, who has time for self-care and doctor appointments? Slap some Vicks on it and get back to it, Momma!

10. The future. Will Junior graduate from your alma mater or be drafted into the climate wars? The future is terrifying, but it'll have to wait—you've got enough on your plate for today.

INTRODUCTION • 17

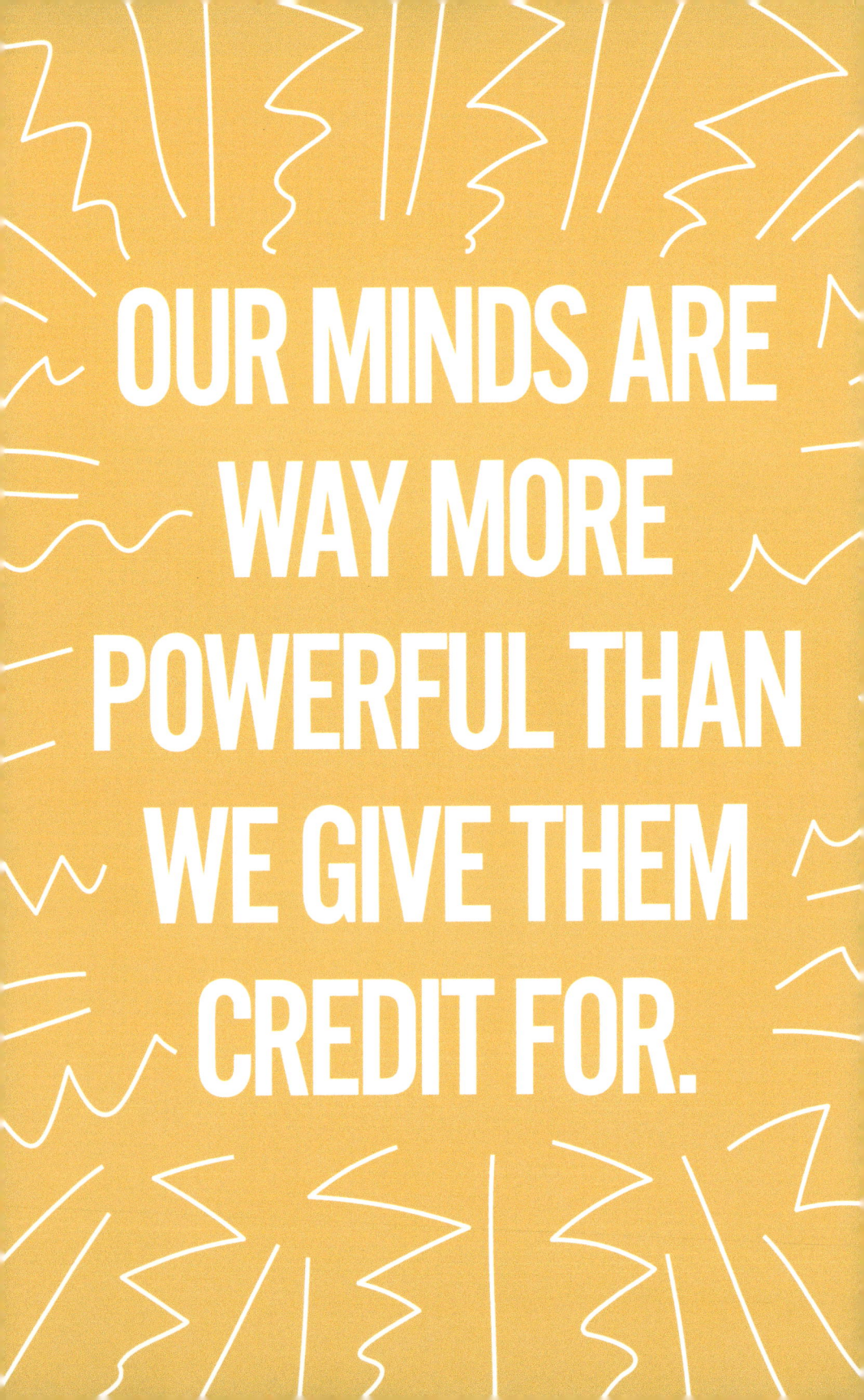

CHAPTER 1
MEET NOISE

I once had an acquaintance who seemed to be a magnet for bad luck. She was constantly complaining, but to me it seemed justified: she truly did have a lot to complain about. Her car was always breaking down; her relationships always ended in disappointment; restaurants got her order wrong on a regular basis. She seemed to think she was cursed and, after knowing her for some time, I started to wonder if she had a point.

But the more time I spent with this acquaintance, the more I had to consider whether she was a passive victim of circumstance or an active master of her own fate. I posit that her continuous focus on negativity had triggered a constant stream of pitfalls in her life. It seemed she had effectively tapped into the power of the mind—but in a harmful way.

THE POWER OF THE MIND

As soon as we wake up in the morning, there are already thousands of thoughts swirling around in our heads. They range from things we want to do to things we *have* to do: pick up the dry cleaning, feed the dog, take the kids to baseball, pay the plumber. A single thought has the power to control our emotions, our behaviors, and even our physical health.

Imagine you're driving to work in the morning when you realize you forgot your son's baseball mitt at home. This realization affects your emotions: you're upset with yourself for forgetting, anxious about missing your morning meeting, and frustrated that your son's mitt is somehow *your* responsibility. It affects your behavior, making you drive faster than normal and maybe even curse out a driver or two as you speed by. And surely that cortisol spike from the stress you're experiencing affects your health. All of that follows from a single, neutral thought: *I forgot my son's mitt at home.*

Our minds are way more powerful than we give them credit for. Thoughts are like magnets, attracting circumstances and responses to themselves. After all, like attracts like, thought attracts thought, and noise attracts noise. This means that what we fixate on does, in fact, become our reality. If you constantly think things aren't working out, they'll continue to go wrong. The deeper you fall down this negative rabbit hole, the less aware of other possibilities you become.

GIVE US THIS DAY OUR DAILY NOISE

If we're not aware, noise has the potential to derail our day from the moment we open our eyes in the morning.

Think about how it feels to sleep through your alarm on a workday. You scramble to get dressed, gobble down breakfast, grab a quick coffee, and make a mad dash for work. All the while, your mind is racing with negative thoughts: *Why didn't anyone wake me up? Why did I stay up so late last night? Why does everything always seem to go wrong?* It's barely 8 a.m. and you're already on a treadmill of noise that threatens to derail your entire day.

Now compare that to a day when you woke up before your alarm. You got dressed, ate a balanced breakfast, sang along to your favorite playlist in the car, and even had time to swing by the deli to grab a sandwich for lunch. Sounds ideal, right? What if you could wake up late and still experience the inner peace of a leisurely morning?

"But Angelina," you might say, "you haven't met my boss! It's only logical to panic." Sure, you may face consequences for arriving late. But maybe you won't. Maybe your boss is working from home today, or at a meeting off-site; maybe she's stuck in traffic herself. Maybe none of those things are true and she simply doesn't care as much as you think she does!

In any case, reacting as though the worst-case scenario is the only possible outcome won't help you get to work any quicker. Neither will punishing yourself for running behind. Your lateness may be a fact, but the noise that accompanies it isn't. It's just noise.

Rather than allow an alarm clock to dictate our moods, we have to learn to rely on the power of our thoughts. When I sleep through my alarm and wake up in a hysterical state—which, as a mother of three, could easily be my norm—I quickly attempt to regroup and redirect my thoughts toward positivity. When I'm able to do this, the quality of my day no longer depends on whether I woke up before or after my alarm.

> **QUICK TIP** *The next time you're running late and about to panic, take a deep breath and say to yourself: "I'm late today. How will I feel about that a week from now?" More likely than not, your being late is so insignificant in the grand scheme of things that you'll never think about it again—so why let it derail your day?*

If you begin the day in emotional chaos, how can you possibly hear your own happiness, let alone attend to it? That's why it's incredibly important to pause and assess our thought patterns. Are we living a life focused on happiness, or noise?

DEFINING NOISE

Now that you've met noise, let's define it.

> **Noise** [noiz]; *noun*
>
> 1. anything that detracts from happiness
> 2. a roadblock to happiness, manifesting in social, emotional, or physical form
> 3. a state of chaos
> 4. a negative reaction to experiences, memories, people, or situations
> 5. a reversible circumstance that can be blocked to achieve happiness

We're all surrounded by noise. How many text messages, emails, push notifications, or phone calls have interrupted you since you started reading this book? How many do you receive daily, as you go about your routine? It's probably impossible to add them all up. And let's not even get into the time it takes to prioritize and respond to every beep and buzz vying for your attention!

While modern life is noisy, not all noise is detrimental to our happiness. Some of it adds to our lives, like a happy birthday message from a loved one. And while paying the bills is pretty much no one's idea of fun, it's possible to accept it as part of our routine (especially if we enjoy modern luxuries like running water). In other words, noise, like happiness, is personal. That's why it's important that we learn to delineate between what adds to our personal happiness and what we need to limit or block in order to protect our peace.

THE THREE TYPES OF NOISE

In order to recognize our own noise, we need to understand the masks it wears. Most noise falls into one of three categories: social, emotional, and physical.

Social Noise

Social noise is one we all deal with on multiple levels. It can come from the ingrained societal beliefs and traditions of those around us, or it can be a result of our relationships with others—specifically, the social roles we play.

In our attempts to live up to the social role of "mother," for example, what should be a source of happiness easily becomes a source of guilt, anxiety, and fatigue. We find ourselves consumed with caretaking, unable to honor the gift of motherhood for what it is. The beauty of the mother-child relationship is overshadowed by the noise telling us there's still more to do—and to do it better than before. It's overshadowed by societal or cultural beliefs about how moms should "be": everything from how we dress to the types of relationships we're allowed to have. Without even realizing it, we push everything about us that isn't "mom-friendly" to the dark corners of our mind until we forget the complexity of who we are.

While society offers us plenty of roles to measure ourselves against, we also create our own images to live up to. The incentives on social media encourage us to present ourselves not as we are, but as an amplification or projection of who we think we should be. We're not Nancy; we're the Proud and Effortless Mother of Twins. We're not Sonia; we're the Mother of Five with the Magical Rock-Hard Abs. As we post our filtered pictures and make claims about our lives, we create an idealized version of ourselves in real time. It's hard enough to live up to our own expectations in the real world; it's exponentially harder to live up to a digitally fashioned ideal we've created for the sole purpose of impressing others.

> **QUICK TIP** *Stop negatively labeling yourself! You are not a Worrier, you have a negative emotional habit that can be broken. Avoid thinking of and introducing yourself according to noisy emotional habits. Substitute the negative with the positive. Try: "I am kind" instead of "I'm a Worrier."*

Emotional Noise

Emotional noise comes in the form of negative emotional habits. Worry is one example I'm sure we all know too well. Many of us assume that if we worry about something to excess, we'll be better prepared to deal with it when it happens. And the media does a great job of assuring us that, whatever it is, it *will* happen. No parent can watch the news or check social media without being offered five new reasons to keep their kids indoors until they turn eighteen.

But imagine you have a next-door neighbor who binge-watches the news 24/7 for potential terrorist threats—would you consider that healthy? Necessary? No. Logically, we all know that hypervigilance doesn't make you more prepared, it just makes you more anxious. People who worry don't have an easier time dealing with life than people who don't. Your extra worry is unnecessary emotional noise. The more time you spend worrying, the less time you have for happiness.

Social media is a common source of emotional noise. Baked into our daily routines are emotions like jealousy, resentment, and shame as we absent-mindedly scroll through curated snapshots of other people's lives.

Research shows that viewing a post for even a split second can trigger harmful thought patterns: *I don't measure up; I'm not good enough; I'm missing out; I will never have enough.* Having a front-row seat to your nephew scoring the winning goal, the new additions to your neighbor's home, and your favorite momfluencer's sixteenth glamorous vacation this year is enough to make anyone feel like they're on the outside looking in, regardless of how much they have going for them in reality. The more we focus on what we don't have, the less we appreciate all we *do* have—and the noisier we become.

Physical Noise

Physical noise comes in the form of self-defeating thoughts about our bodies, our environments, and our relationships with self-care. I know so many moms who struggle to put themselves first, regardless of how desperately they need a break. If you're reading this book, you might be one of them. But what if I told you that taking care of yourself is a way to take care of others? That when we take care of ourselves first, we become better parents, spouses, employees, children, siblings, and friends?

Airplanes offer us an unexpected lesson on the importance of self-care. From the flight attendant to the in-cabin instructional videos and laminated safety cards placed in perfectly unavoidable positions, we can't ignore the warning that, in the event of an emergency, we must put on our own masks first before helping others. This seemingly innocuous public service announcement holds a universal truth: to properly take care of others, you must take care of yourself first.

The idea of taking care of ourselves first doesn't just feel impractical; it can even feel immoral. As a society, we're taught from a young age to think of others, to do what's right for the group, to be a team player. Our lives can quickly become consumed by taking care of everyone around us—except us. We prioritize our children, our spouses, our extended families, our bosses, our co-workers, and our friends. The list of priorities is endless, and more often than not we find ourselves at the bottom.

While we do receive fulfillment, meaning, and value from taking care of others, we run the risk of depleting ourselves, leaving us exhausted, overwhelmed, unfulfilled, and resentful. We must be conscious of the balance between supporting the people in our lives and taking care of ourselves.

THE NOISE COMING FROM INSIDE THE HOUSE

While some noise is obvious to us—commercials hawking bottled happiness, the woman in our mommy group who's constantly one-upping us, the hundreds of spam emails overtaking our inbox—some noise is more difficult to identify.

The expectations we place on ourselves are some of the most insidious examples of noise: *Get straight A's. Get promoted. Be a good friend. Make your spouse happy. Save enough for your children's education. Break the internet with your next 'gram.*

We're so fixated on meeting these goals that we often fail to notice they're making us miserable, adding all kinds of stress and pressure to our lives that only detracts from our happiness. Rather than take all of our thoughts and goals at face value, we need to make a habit of sifting through them, salvaging what promotes our happiness and discarding the rest.

Noise can also invade our happiest moments. I know the anticipation and excitement one feels before becoming a parent by choice. You can't wait until your child is born. Their future arrival elicits an inner happiness so extraordinary, it feels otherworldly, even out-of-body.

You want to preserve, foster, and nurture that feeling forever. But as you gaze at your newborn, the noise suddenly creeps in. You don't want to pay it any mind, but you can't help it. *Is my baby healthy? Will I be a good parent? How will I pay for college? Will they make the right choices?* All the excitement dissipates—but it shouldn't. Those feelings are noisy. Why not hold on to that feeling of promise and wonder inherent in being a parent? This is a choice you can make, but only if you realize it's a choice.

WHAT NOISE ISN'T

Before we go deeper, it's important to clarify that trauma is not noise. Historically, trauma was defined as "a deeply distressing or disturbing experience." However, recent research has deepened our understanding: What sets traumatic experiences apart from other challenging experiences is the ongoing—and often debilitating—emotional responses that result from them. In other words, what makes an experience traumatic is not just the nature of the event itself, but the lasting emotional impact that event has on us.

Trauma can take many forms, but some of the most common risk factors are outlined by the Adverse Childhood Experiences (ACE) scale. They include neglect, physical abuse, emotional abuse, sexual abuse, having an incarcerated relative, household dysfunction, domestic violence, mental illness, and substance abuse.

It's important to note that this list is not exhaustive, nor is it definitive. There are many events that can result in trauma that aren't listed above, and a person can experience an ACE event without developing trauma responses. Trauma, like happiness, is highly personal. However, if you have experienced one or more event on the ACE scale and struggle with one or more of the following symptoms, you may benefit from additional support as you learn to block the noise:

Trauma Indicators

- Severe anxiety and/or depression
- Flashbacks
- Nightmares
- Difficulty functioning in daily life
- Insomnia
- Fatigue
- Intrusive thoughts
- Chronic pain
- Challenges managing emotions (mood swings, hopelessness, irritability, pervasive anger)
- Difficulty connecting with others

While noise is not trauma, trauma can cause noise. Noise is like the tip of an iceberg you can spot from the ocean's shore, while the cause of the noise—the real source of negativity in your life—is the invisible mass lurking beneath the surface. We often can't see that there's a huge structure supporting the tip of the iceberg until we dive into the depths of the water. For some people, that structure is trauma; for others, it may be a lack of self-esteem or an unexamined fear from childhood. Whatever the source, we can't block the noise without addressing the invisible structures that support it.

If you've not yet taken steps to address past trauma, you may struggle to practice the ideas in this book. That's because traumatic experiences can lead to chronic noise. For those who've experienced trauma, negative thoughts are not just an occasional issue but a persistent, controlling, and debilitating filter that distorts reality. When I began my journey to happiness, I realized my noisy thoughts often originated from my own traumatic experiences. In order to block the noise, I had to recognize the control those past experiences had on my present-day thoughts, behaviors, and emotions and reclaim that control. True healing came when I was able to work through the trauma while being conscious of the ways it was manifesting in my daily life.

Of course, my experiences with trauma are unique to me. Just as there's no one-size-fits-all solution for happiness, there's no "normal" way to respond to, or recover from, traumatic experiences. Again, trauma is deeply personal; the impact it has on you will be just as unique as your path forward. That's why it's so important not to judge or compare yourself with others as you embark on this journey: two people can go through the same experiences and have very different responses. Therefore, there's no "right" way to heal from trauma—there's only what's right for you.

Even if you don't have a traumatic past, I cannot stress enough that this journey requires you to show yourself great gentleness and patience. Don't hold yourself to an impossible standard of perfection or compare yourself with others. Your journey is yours alone—and while it may be a long one, it doesn't have to be a lone one. If you need to speak to a therapist, spiritual adviser, healer, physician, or trusted loved one, I encourage and empower you to do so. It's often the biggest sign of strength to not only recognize you need help but to enlist and engage it.

Despite what you may have witnessed or experienced in the past, you already contain within you everything you need to live your best life. I truly believe that, because I've lived it. It all comes down to this: you have control over your life. Maybe you haven't always taken ownership of it, but this book exists to show you how you can.

It is time to be unapologetically, wholeheartedly you.

THE VOLUME OF NOISE

Happiness is quiet. It's calm. It's inside all of us, but it's impossible to hear it when it's under a thick layer of noise.

Noise is the opposite of quiet. It's loud and demanding. Noise is like the boisterous, draining auntie you see only at Thanksgiving—the one you want to ignore but who somehow ends up talking your ear off all afternoon.

Is it any wonder many of us focus on noise by default? The noise of our responsibilities, tasks, and obligations is like a whirlwind whipping us around, day in and day out. By the time we've answered all the bells and put out all the fires, we don't have the time or energy to attend to our happiness.

Since it's human nature to have both happy and noisy thoughts, we must consciously choose which to focus on. Fortunately, we *do* have a choice in the matter. When all you hear is noise, look for the happiness buried beneath it. It's already there; you just need to change course and move toward it.

WHAT WOULD YOUR INNER CHILD DO?

While noise may be a new concept to you, you've actually had the ability to block it for as long as you've been able to speak. Children have a natural knack for choosing happiness over noise—it's something they do almost automatically.

My own children often act as a litmus test for how balanced I am between happiness and noise. I love planning my children's birthday parties. Every time they roll around, I go into full party-planning mode. But I just as quickly become overwhelmed by the need to include everyone. So each year, I invite every member of my kid's current grade, and their previous grades, and all of our family friends, too. These parties are huge events. The screeching and chaos of the overflowing bouncy castle is forever imprinted in my mind.

When my oldest was about to turn eight, he looked me in the eyes and said, "Mom, I really don't enjoy these big birthday parties you throw for me. I just want to invite my five close friends, play, have pizza, and watch a movie."

He had no inhibitions about what he wanted. He didn't feel any guilt about not inviting the entire class. He wanted to spend his birthday with the people who mattered to him most, and he didn't second-guess it. It was eye-opening for me—he'd blocked the social noise without wavering. That's the way to happiness. Children don't get caught up in social expectations and the self-inflicted guilt of not meeting them. Suffice to say, I was proud of his wisdom and honesty. He embodies happiness. As for me, I am a work in progress and have planned many unnecessarily large parties.

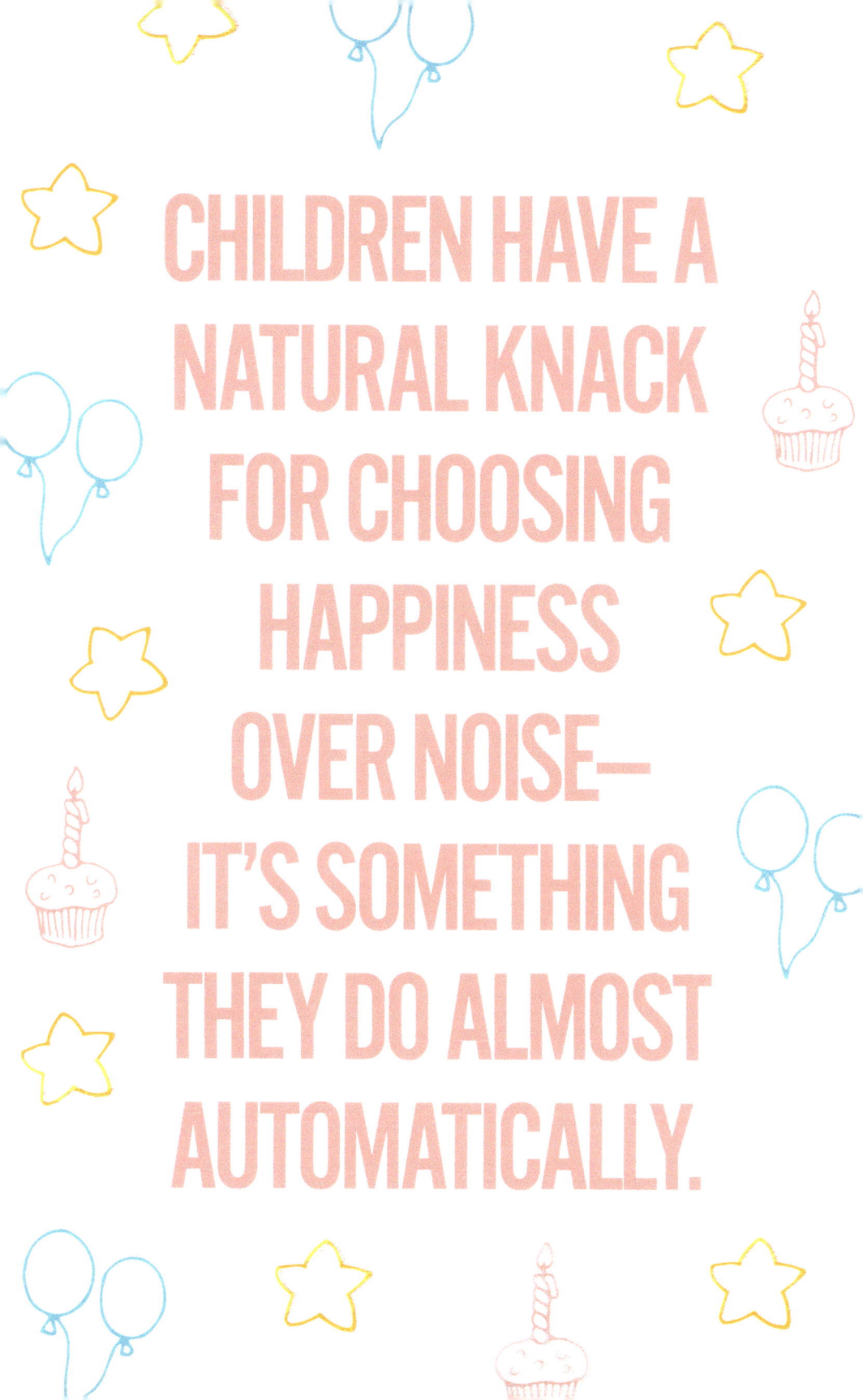

CHILDREN HAVE A NATURAL KNACK FOR CHOOSING HAPPINESS OVER NOISE— IT'S SOMETHING THEY DO ALMOST AUTOMATICALLY.

WE ALL WANT TO BE SEEN AND ACCEPTED FOR EVERYTHING WE ARE.

CHAPTER 2
PLAYING OUR ROLES

One of my all-time favorite movies is the John Hughes classic *The Breakfast Club*. If you're not familiar, the film centers on five high school students who are sentenced to Saturday detention by their uptight vice principal. While their infractions are initially a mystery, we're able to make assumptions about each student immediately—assumptions that are reinforced, and then challenged, as the day wears on.

Even before a single word is exchanged among the teens, we know they inhabit different social roles. We can tell by how (or if) they interacted with their parents that morning, what cars they arrived in, their aesthetics, even their body language. Our impressions are further cemented by how they interact with the vice principal, and then with each other.

For example, no one is surprised when the leather-clad, cigarette-smoking rebel shows up to serve his time. But what did the soft-spoken, studious kid do to warrant Saturday detention? And what about the golden-boy jock and the pretty-in-pink princess—how'd they end up here? Perhaps most perplexing is the unpredictable outlier, if only because she's nonverbal for most of the film.

But as the teens alternate between making assumptions, accusations, and confessions, it dawns on them—and us—that they're more than the stereotypes assigned to them. By telling their stories, they discover that, stripped of the roles they play for their families and friends, they have far more in common than their appearances would suggest.

I love this film, because it speaks to a very real and painful dilemma many of us face throughout our lives. We all want to be seen and accepted for everything we are—yet we also feel pressure to commit to a certain role, to play a part that can be easily understood by others.

Think about it: when you meet someone new, what question is almost guaranteed to come up in the first five minutes? I'm sure you know. It's the dreaded "And what do you do?" The question that requires us to distill everything we are into digestible cocktail-party sound bites. In the West, this is how we're taught to define and value ourselves—not by who we are, but by what we do.

While no one likes being stereotyped or mislabeled, we still tend to feel lost when we don't have a role to play. I fell into this trap often when I first made the shift from full-time researcher to full-time mother. Without the tangible milestones of an active career—a new research topic, my latest publication—my kids became the "proof" that I was still contributing something of value to the world.

In this way, my kids' accomplishments became a reflection of my own. If my children were happy, healthy, and successful, I was a good mom. And I believed I needed to be a good mom—no, a fantastic one—if I wanted to justify my choice to leave academia.

Of course, that's not what I was thinking as I signed my kids up for a billion and one activities or threw them extravagant parties they didn't want. I wasn't nearly so calculated. I just knew that when my kids were happy, so was I. But if and when they weren't? Well, then I had to question my entire existence!

If you've ever met a toddler, you know that basing your self-worth and identity on their moods is a recipe for disaster. But I wasn't really thinking of myself; rather, I was drowning in the noise of what I thought a mother should do. Eventually I would discover that what made me feel like a "good" mom and what made my kids happy were often not the same thing. In fact, by laser-focusing on this one aspect of my identity, I was inadvertently sending my kids the message that what we *do* is more valuable than who we *are*.

WHO ARE WE?

If I were to ask you to describe yourself, there's a high probability you would list off the "roles" you play before your personal traits. We often find it easier to say "I'm a [parent, child, sibling, friend, colleague, coach, etc.]" than to acknowledge that we're funny, energetic, athletic, kind, or adventurous.

But we have this tendency to define ourselves by our relationships not because we don't know ourselves, but because we know ourselves all too well. Humans are social beings. From the moment we wake up to the time we go to sleep, we're interacting with people, even if they're only with us in our thoughts. To understand ourselves, it's vital that we understand our relationships and how they shape who we are.

When we hear the word "relationship," some of us default to thinking of our romantic partner (or lack thereof). Others think first of the relationship that demands the most time, consideration, and effort. While it's undeniable that some relationships are more influential or meaningful to us than others, it's also undeniable that we're entwined in far more relationships than those that first spring to mind. It's important to examine all our roles and relationships, because each of them brings a unique aspect of ourselves to the surface. If we discount relationships that we deem less important, we lose valuable information about who we are—and about the sources of noise in our lives.

Here's a non-exhaustive list of common roles. Make note of the ones you play in your various relationships, including any that might be missing from this list:

Common Social Roles

- Parent
- Stepparent
- Grandparent
- Spouse
- Partner
- Girlfriend/boyfriend
- Ex
- Cousin
- Aunt/uncle
- Niece/nephew
- Co-worker
- Colleague
- Employer
- Employee
- Manager
- Mentor
- Mentee
- Friend
- Acquaintance
- Bandmate
- Coach
- Teacher
- Student
- Captain
- Competitor
- Neighbor
- _____
- _____

We've already seen how noisy things can become when we lean too far into one role. Now let's explore a few other common ways our relationships inadvertently create noise in our lives.

CHOOSING FAMILIAR OVER HAPPY

We all know someone who "married his mother." That's because many of us are unconsciously, magnetically drawn to what we know—whether it's healthy or not. It's easy to be attracted to a noisy dynamic when it's familiar and comfortable.

Now, I'm not saying it's a bad sign when your partner reminds you of Mom or Dad. Some of us even dream of finding someone who's just like a beloved parent. But that yearning for the familiar works both ways. If your parents constantly bickered in front of you, for example, you might have internalized the idea that squabbling is a legit love language. Or you might grow to avoid conflict altogether, allowing your partner to trample all over you or fleeing at the first sign of discord.

It's not that we should never, ever date anyone who reminds us of our parents—but we do need to know that what we perceive as "normal" isn't always going to make us happy. The only way to avoid falling for the familiar-but-noisy is to be conscious of our relationship choices. Have we seen this pattern before? Is it enriching or depleting us? Remember: happiness is a choice—and if we're used to noise, it might be a difficult one to make. The good news is, like all things, it gets easier with practice.

A REASON, A SEASON, A LIFETIME

When I was eight, I had a wonderful group of friends. We'd go back and forth between one another's houses, spending countless hours planning our futures and sharing our deepest secrets. My childhood was molded and enriched by these friends; even all these years later, I still treasure the formative years we spent together. But the fact is that as we grew older, our needs, desires, and interests evolved in different directions. The roles we once played perfectly for one another no longer fit.

As the poet Brian A. "Drew" Chalker wrote, "People come into your life for a reason, a season, or a lifetime." Some relationships really are forever, evolving and changing at just the right pace. Some are circumstantial, temporary, and not all that impactful, while others are brief yet incredibly profound. There are those who travel alongside us for the long haul and those who simply point us in the right direction.

But recognizing when a relationship no longer suits us is just half the battle—actually letting go can be much more challenging. There are so many difficult emotions that keep us invested in relationships that no longer serve us: loyalty, fear, loneliness, guilt. We recognize that we want to grow, but we're still trying to live up to outdated expectations and perceptions—and that tension creates near-constant noise, making inner peace all but impossible.

That's because people—and relationships—are complicated. The same friend who's a source of guidance, information, support, and comfort can also be a source of frustration, anxiety, concern, and obligation. Relationships are rarely all or nothing; instead, they're a complex pastiche of happiness and noise. We'll review strategies for managing this noise later; for now, just know that it's perfectly normal for it to creep into even the best relationships. What matters most is how we respond.

A CASE OF BAD VIBES

Early in my career, I had a wonderful colleague who was a great source of support. But for some reason, I was very anxious around them—not to mention irritable, short-tempered, and overwhelmed. To make matters worse, I felt terrible about feeling terrible. Why was I reacting so negatively to someone who was seemingly quite helpful?

I'll never forget the day we stopped working together—I was literally whistling. The thing is, my former colleague wasn't even ostensibly noisy. But, for whatever reason, our relationship brought out something unhealthy in me. It was truly an "It's not you, it's me" situation. In analyzing the relationship, I recognized that while my colleague wasn't noisy, *I* was becoming noisy in their presence. And that was enough to warrant change.

ANALYZING YOUR RELATIONSHIP ROLES

Exploring your relationship roles is an amazing way to gain clarity on what's going right (and wrong) in your world. When I analyzed my role as a mother, it was nothing short of an epiphany. By doing so, I was able to see how I was allowing my kids' moods—and how vigilantly I tended to them—to determine my self-worth. In short, I'd been depending on others to determine my value—and, more importantly, my happiness. While I love my children more than anything, I know my happiness can't depend on theirs. Moreover, by revolving our happiness around the triumphs or defeats of our loved ones, we can easily convey the message that they are responsible for our emotional well-being. Such a responsibility is unfair and damaging.

Many parents are all too familiar with the feeling that we are exactly as happy as our unhappiest child. Admittedly, I have fallen victim to this experience more than I care to remember. When we learn to block the noise, we are able to empathize without sacrifice. We can love, support, and care for our family and friends while safeguarding our happiness all at the same time. Hopefully, you're beginning to see the value of analyzing the various roles you play in your relationships. It can be an eye-opening exercise, bringing vague recurring themes and patterns into sharper focus. When we consciously understand our roles—and the noise inherent in them—we can choose differently.

Before you dive in, let's cover some ground rules:

Analysis does not equal judgment. As you begin the process of analyzing your relationships, be careful not to engage in self-criticism, degradation, or judgment. Your relationships—and all their good, bad, and ugly—made you who you are. This exercise is meant to help you explore where you've been and how you reached this point, not give you permission to beat yourself up.

There are no mistakes, just lessons. Instead of dwelling on what you could have done differently, celebrate all that you've learned in the process of becoming you.

Treat yourself and your journey with unconditional love. There's no such thing as selectively loving yourself. It's all or nothing.

Now, let's get started!

EXERCISE: PLAYING OUR ROLES

Open a fresh page in your notebook (or a fresh Excel spreadsheet, if that's more your style) and create five columns:

In **COLUMN A**, write down all the relationship roles you play. Use the list from earlier in this chapter to get started, but feel free to expand on it to include all the roles that are important to you.

Next to each role, in **COLUMN B**, write the names of the people in your life who interact with you in that role. You may play more than one role with the same person—for example, with a friend who's also your bandmate. In that case, list the name next to all relevant roles.

Next, in **COLUMN C**, work your way down the list, describing each relationship in terms of the ways in which your life is impacted by noise. In what ways is this relationship noisy, and in what ways is it quiet and happy? Write down what comes to mind immediately, then return to each entry after more thoughtful exploration, adding detail and examples. Fight the urge to edit your initial impulses and, whatever you do, don't delete anything! Everything that comes up during this step is valuable information.

COLUMN A	COLUMN B	COLUMN C
Parent	Leo and Elle	overwhelmed
Spouse	James	happy
Employer	Kate and Joe	stressed
Friend	Paige and Kelly	relaxed

If nothing comes to mind immediately, use these prompts to help you get started:

- How do I usually feel when we're together?
- How do I usually behave when we're together?
- What interactions between us stand out most in my mind?
- What is the foundation of our connection?

- *What adjectives would I use to describe this person?*
- *Has guilt played a role in this attachment?*
- *Are the memories I hold on to about this person mostly positive or mostly negative?*

In **COLUMN D**, review what you wrote for each relationship one by one and label each relationship "noisy," "noise-free," or a mixture of both. Don't feel guilty about labeling a relationship as "noisy"—family ties are notorious for their noise, and you're not a bad person for noticing. This is your list, and your truth.

Finally, in **COLUMN E**, write down the degree to which this relationship influences your daily life. You can use a five-point system, with 1 being "never" and 5 being "daily." If you're feeling stuck, answer these questions to determine how impacted you are by each relationship:

- *Do I talk to or see this person on a daily basis?*
- *Does our relationship influence daily aspects of my life?*
- *Do I feel supported, encouraged, enriched, and fulfilled by this relationship?*
- *Do I feel emotionally, physically, or mentally exhausted after our interactions?*

COLUMN D	COLUMN E
mix	5
noise-free	5
noisy	4
noise-free	2

- *Does the noise linger for a while after our interactions, or is it fleeting?*
- *Do I feel burdened by the noise, even when we're not interacting?*

Action Item: For one week, dedicate thirty minutes a day to analyzing what all your relationships have in common. Do you tend to play the same role in each relationship? Do your past and/or present partners have similar qualities? Have your relationships changed over time, or have they stayed the same? Note the commonalities in your journal.

COLUMN A	COLUMN B
Relationship role that you play	*People who interact with you*

COLUMN C	COLUMN D	COLUMN E
Relationship description	*Noisy, noise-free, or both*	*Influence on daily life (1-5)*

WE DON'T NEED TO MAKE EXCUSES, CHANGE OUR NAMES, OR MOVE CROSS-COUNTRY TO AVOID THE NOISY PEOPLE IN OUR LIVES.

CHAPTER 3
SAFEGUARDING HAPPINESS

I have fond memories of the pride my mother took in her collection of tea ware. She carefully placed each cup and saucer on display in the mahogany china cabinet she inherited from her dear friend, where they rested until the next special occasion. We all revered this cabinet, because it held what was near and dear to us: our family's story, values, and traditions, passed down from one generation to the next.

After I got married, I had my own wedding china to arrange and display—and my mother and I devoted an entire afternoon to the task. The simple act of delicately placing each plate on display was the beginning of a new tradition in my home, one that celebrated how we show care and appreciation for our precious items.

From a young age, many of us are taught to value our belongings, to treat delicate items with care. Yet we're given no instructions on how to safeguard our happiness. We have more rules for a friend borrowing a shirt than we do for protecting our emotional well-being. Happiness is, in my opinion, the most precious thing we own—so why do so many of us leave it vulnerable to noise?

THE FINE ART OF DETACHMENT

"Detachment" has a bad reputation. The word conjures images of a person who's never really present, someone disconnected from the people around them. It conjures a sense of seclusion, isolation, indifference, and emotional numbness.

But to the contrary, my friends! Detachment is healthy. This practice helps us to protect our emotional, intellectual, physical, and spiritual well-being. It's when we create a physical and/or psychological space to protect our happiness from noise. When we detach, we're not disappearing—we're simply elevating our happiness until it's out of reach. It's like my mother's tea ware: displayed in a place of honor and reverence, where it can be seen but not touched.

Learning the art of detachment can help us foster, maintain, and grow happy relationships. It even allows us to spend time with noisy people—and emerge completely unscathed. That's right: we don't need to make excuses, change our names, or move cross-country to avoid the noisy people in our lives. Who knew?

REJECTION VS. DETACHMENT

I used to have a very "all or nothing" attitude toward relationships. Either they were perfect and worth investing in or they were damaged and required terminating. I had no idea how to eliminate relationship noise without eliminating the entire relationship: at the first hint of noise, I was lacing up my running shoes. I didn't have a single clue about how to enrich a relationship and, as a result, I was on the fast track to Lonely Island.

After many failed relationships, I realized that rejection was not working. Rejection removed the person from my life, but it still left me submerged in noise. *What will they tell people? What if I run into them? Did I do the right thing—and if so, why do I feel so awful?*

Rejection may physically remove people from our world, but it doesn't remove the noise we associate with the relationship—and in many cases it amplifies it. We're often unaware of the toll that cutting people off can take on us. When we reject someone, it may seem like we're in the power position—after all, we did make the call to end things. But in truth, walking away from a significant relationship often leaves us feeling guilty, regretful, and just plain sad. In order to reassure ourselves that we made the right choice, we might begin to discount or deny any positive impact the relationship had on us. And while turning people into villains may help us avoid our difficult feelings in the moment, the relief is temporary, because, deep down, we know it was more complicated than that.

I once knew a woman who'd completely cut off her in-laws because they'd "done her wrong" one too many times. Despite her husband's attempts to set things right, despite her daughters' initial confusion and eventual protests, she was done. When we met, she'd been no-contact with her in-laws for three years—even her husband learned not to bring them up if it wasn't totally necessary—yet she still referenced them in conversation on a regular basis. The relationships were gone, the daily interactions were gone, but the noise, hurt, and anguish remained. Not only that, but her all-or-nothing approach was creating a rift with her children and husband.

LEARNING TO DETACH

If you found yourself relating to this example, don't get down on yourself. You're not alone! Anyone can fall down the slippery slope of rejection. The idea that we can be happy without erasing every less-than-pleasant relationship we're in is not intuitive; it must be learned. Remember: we're taught how to value and preserve our possessions. But our happiness? Not so much. My promise to you is that with detachment, it can be done.

Before we get to that, though, it has to be said: it's crucial that you never attend to abusive relationships, those that are altogether unhealthy, harmful, and hurtful. Noise is not the same thing as verbal, emotional, or physical abuse. If that's what you're experiencing, you *must* remove yourself from the relationship. When abuse is involved, detachment will never be enough. However, it's still a useful tool in that it can help you preserve your emotional wellness and sanity through the difficult process of leaving an unhealthy relationship.

Now, let's run through some FAQs, tools, and mantras that will help you navigate detachment.

1

Question: Am I responsible for my loved one's noisy behavior?

Answer: You are not the cause of someone else's behavior, and you're not responsible for it, either. Someone else's noise (e.g., anger, selfishness, sadness, deceit, hysteria, or anxiety, to name a few) belongs to them, and them alone.

When we think we're responsible for a friend or family member's behavior, our own guilt is often the culprit. *If I only said this or did that, they'd be a different person* is something we've probably all felt at one time or another—the key word being *felt*. The idea that we could've changed our actions to produce the exact result we wanted *in someone else's behavior* isn't empirical. It's not rational. Whether you have reason to feel guilty or not, your guilt is still just a feeling. It's not a fact. You could've said or done the exact right thing (according to you) and still ended up with the same outcome.

Instead of trying to "fix" your relationships and noisy loved ones, consider turning your focus inward. Take a step back and examine your own noise, which is currently telling you that you're responsible for your loved one's behavior. Write down all the reasons you feel responsible for someone else's noise. You'll soon discover that your reasons aren't based in rational thought, but in emotionally charged reactions.

You can be someone's mom, spouse, best friend, boss, or daughter, and your actions will *still* never directly cause theirs. After all, who's responsible for *your* behavior and actions? Is it you or someone else? Regardless of how much input, feedback, support, or encouragement you receive from someone else, hopefully you realize that only you make the final call on how to behave. And all of us have that autonomy over ourselves, even your noisiest loved ones. It's not your job to save people from themselves.

Guilt is noisy. It stops us from properly attending to our relationships, because we can't see the people in them for who they really are. We can't see that they're capable of making their own decisions, even if they're decisions we disagree with. We take their noise personally, when it actually has very little to do with us.

To remove guilt from our relationships, we need to take responsibility for our own behavior—no more and no less. We need to relinquish the responsibility we feel for other people's noise. After all, we've got our own lifetime of noise to deal with!

Adopt this mantra: **"I will love you for who you are, but I won't be connected to your noise."**

2. Question: Can I change my loved one's noisy behavior?

Answer: The support group Al-Anon was founded for those with loved ones who are struggling with substance abuse. They have a mantra called the Three Cs, and I think it's an important one when dealing with a noisy loved one: you didn't **cause** it, you can't **control** it, and you can't **cure** it. Trying to change someone else's behavior is like trying to steer their car while driving your own. It can't be done. That's a universal truth.

What you can do is learn the practice of acceptance. I learned a lot about acceptance when my own loved one was struggling with substance abuse. For years, I did everything in my power to help her. I connected her with doctors, nutritionists, physical therapists, acupuncturists—you name it, I tried it. I spent many sleepless nights and anxiety-ridden days attempting to change her. When she achieved those hard-won moments of sobriety, I celebrated—not only were they a triumph for her; they were a triumph for me. Now I could finally live—she had changed! Sadly, the sober moments never seemed to last; her illness would return as quickly as it left. And so did my misery.

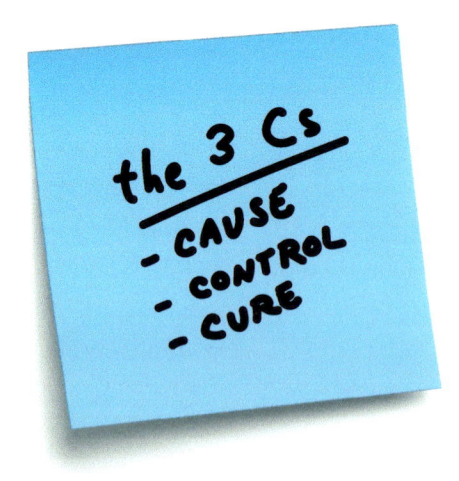

the 3 Cs
- *CAUSE*
- *CONTROL*
- *CURE*

What saved me from being swallowed up by the noise was acceptance. I had to accept her for who she was—illness and all. I could not control her destiny. I had to realize that she wasn't just in the driver's seat of her life, she was on her own road—and so was I, if I chose it. Acceptance freed me from living her life and allowed me to start living my own. My happiness and sanity were no longer contingent on her sobriety. In fact, my happiness has nothing to do with her. I was and am free to live a noise-free life while still maintaining a loving relationship with her. I accept her for who she is, not who I want her to be.

Adopt this mantra: "I accept you for who you are and will no longer attempt to change you."

3 **Question: Can I change how I react to relationship noise?**

Answer: It doesn't matter how you react to noise—that you're reacting at all is the issue. Let's break this down. When you're reactive, you can't be proactive. To react is to let someone else's mood or behavior determine how you feel. When you're proactive, you determine how you're going to *respond* to certain behaviors, people, or situations, before they even happen.

Let's imagine you're at a big family reunion, getting ready to sit down for dinner. You scan the table for a seat as everything goes slow-motion, à la Keanu Reeves in *The Matrix*. There's an open seat next to your favorite cousin and you dash toward it—just as your aunt sits down. You can't tell Auntie to move; she has a bad hip. There's another seat open, next to your uncle. He used to bring you ice cream as a kid, and you decide you can deal with all his Tiger Woods talk. It's not so bad. You begin moving toward him, but then your dad sits down. You certainly can't ask him to move. That's his brother.

There's one last seat open, and it's next to your great-aunt—the cat lady who's overly critical of your parenting style. But instead of gritting your teeth and thinking about how your cat cousins might be orphans by the end of this meal, you take your seat calmly, knowing you've taken the following steps:

Manage Your Expectations. If you know you're going to be rubbing elbows with noisy people, expect noise! Rather than engage in wishful thinking and get blindsided, let experience be your guide. Sure, people can change—but it's better to assume they haven't, and be pleasantly surprised, than to hope otherwise and be disappointed and unprepared.

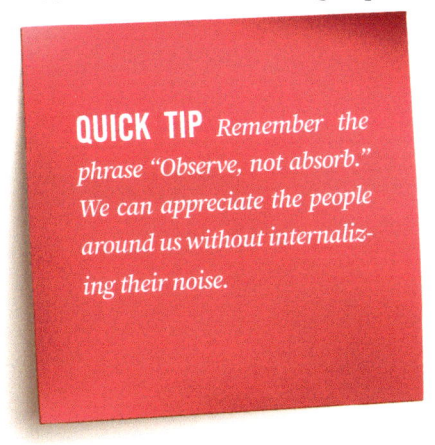

QUICK TIP *Remember the phrase "Observe, not absorb." We can appreciate the people around us without internalizing their noise.*

To make your expectations more concrete, try to anticipate the kind of noise you can expect from the noisy person in question. Exactly how does that great-aunt press your buttons? Maybe it's the endless cat talk, or perhaps it's the breastfeeding advice from the 1950s. Whatever it is, naming it puts you in a better position to recognize it as soon as it starts happening—and to detach accordingly.

Prepare. When you're interacting with a noisy person, your best line of offense is to keep it light. Before an interaction, brainstorm a couple of noise-free topics so that you can engage without things getting heated. Note that what makes a topic noise-free is completely subjective: talking about pets might work with some folks, but it's a topic you want to avoid with your great-aunt. Recommending that new shopping app you love is innocent enough, until you're talking to someone who's drowning in debt. When you anticipate the kind of noise you're going to encounter, you can better prepare to steer the conversation.

Accommodations. Once you're prepared for any unpleasant run-ins, you can make further accommodations to limit noisy interactions. I think of accommodation as the personal concierge of blocking the noise. Before interacting with a noisy person, consider the steps you can take to ensure your time with this person is enjoyable. How long can you realistically be around this person before you start feeling reactive? Set a time limit. Arrive late, or plan to leave early (make sure to let your host know). Bring a neutral party who can act as a buffer. And clock the bathrooms and exits, just in case.

> *Adopt this mantra:* "E (expectation), P (preparation), A (accommodation) before I begin each day."

4 Question: What if I'm attracted to relationship noise?

Answer: You're not alone. Many of us have relationships that are nearly bubbling over with noise. For some of us, relationship noise is the standard—to the extent that wanting to eliminate it makes us feel guilty. What's a relationship without all the noise? Hopefully you're excited to find out. Realizing that you can have noise-free relationships is the first step in breaking a cycle that you've likely been caught in longer than you realize.

Let's revisit the common themes you identified during your relationship analysis. What behaviors and/or personalities are you drawn to? What do these behaviors/personalities do for you? Why do you want to detach from such behaviors/personalities?

If you haven't already, add any old but significant connections to your relationship chart. It's easier to recognize noisy relationships in hindsight, once you're emotionally removed from them. Identify possible links between past and present relationships, and pay special attention to formative relationships—those ties that made a deep early impression on you. Remember: we tend to seek what's familiar, even if it's not good for us.

Consider how relationship noise makes you feel . . . and be honest. We often don't recognize that our connection to a noisy partner provides us with a sense of purpose, control, and power. These relationships make us feel needed—and, perhaps most enticing, they give us the opportunity to ignore our own pain. In other words, they make us feel like heroes while giving us permission to ignore our own mess. As a result, we tend not to recognize how damaging this noise is to our mental and physical well-being.

Seeing the noise on paper will help you identify the type(s) you're most attracted and vulnerable to. By becoming conscious of this, you'll be better equipped to recognize it in new connections. What used to be a green light becomes a red flag.

> *Adopt this mantra:* **"Detachment is not rejection; it is love for myself and appreciation for those I love."**

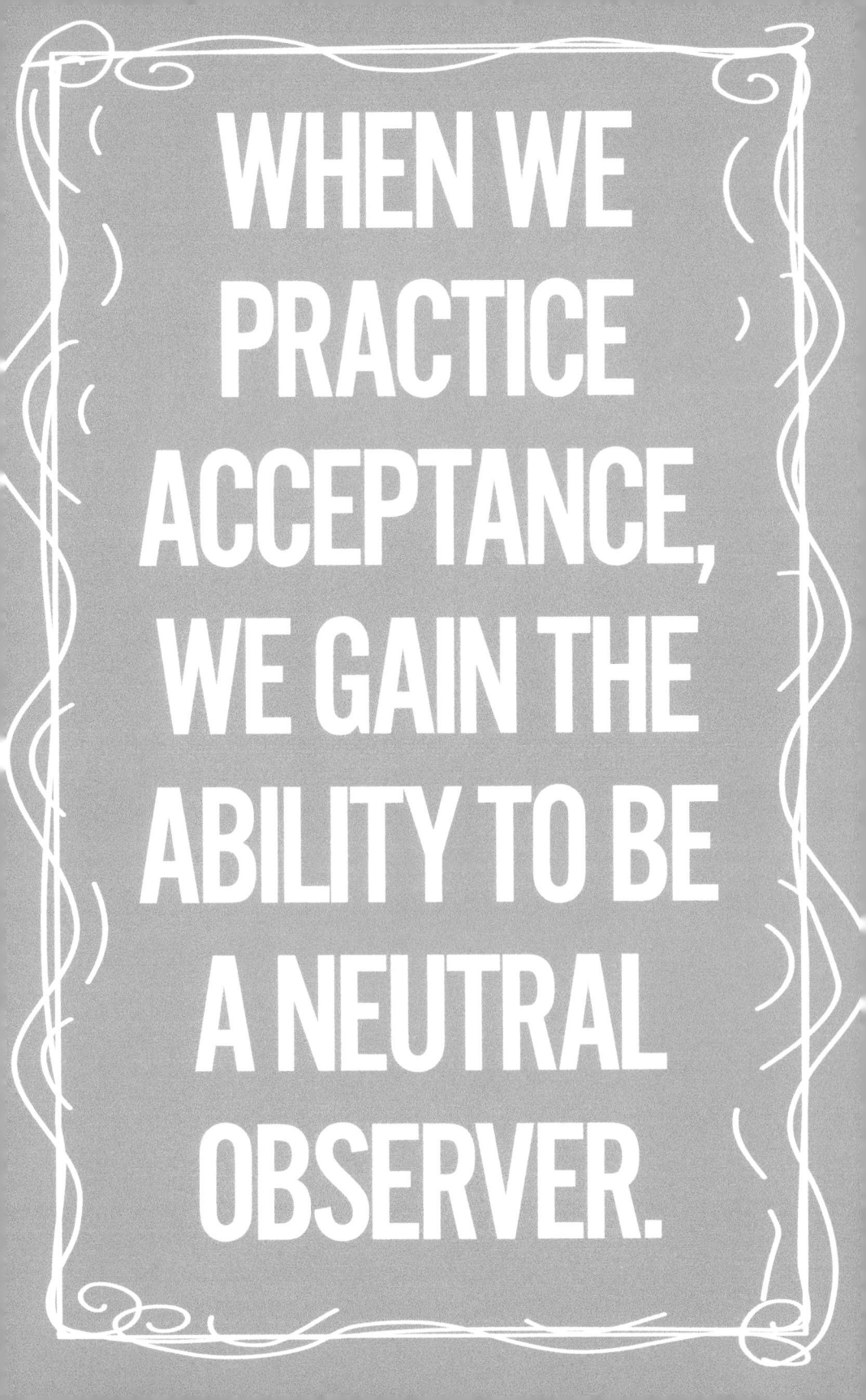

WHEN WE PRACTICE ACCEPTANCE, WE GAIN THE ABILITY TO BE A NEUTRAL OBSERVER.

CHAPTER 4
MASTERING THE ART OF ACCEPTANCE

Have you ever had a friend who'd go on and on about how difficult her mother is? The way she tells it, the woman is straight-up irredeemable. But then you meet Mommy Dearest and, instead of finding a monster, she's actually perfectly pleasant. You're hard-pressed to see the faults and flaws your friend finds so intolerable. What is girlfriend on about?

Yet when the tables are turned—when it's your friends laughing at your mother's bad jokes while you sulk and wonder when they're going to notice the ludicrous way she cuts her steak—it's a whole different story.

Why do we accept our friend's imperfect mother, but not our own? Because it's much easier to accept someone when you don't have a lifetime of memories, experiences, and narratives coloring your every interaction. That's where acceptance comes into play. Acceptance is our ability to recognize the existence of another's noise without feeling the need to take responsibility for it. When we practice acceptance, we gain the ability to be a neutral observer—even in our most intimate relationships.

WHAT IS ACCEPTANCE?

Acceptance can be summed up by one of my favorite sayings: "Let go and let God." It's that quiet and calm moment of clarity that washes over us when we understand what we can and cannot change. It's making peace with what's in our control and what isn't. Acceptance is the acknowledgment that we can't change someone else's noise; we can only change how we respond to it. Acceptance is recognizing that our personal power has limits—and that's exactly as it should be.

Because, paradoxically, when we're able to recognize the limitations of our own power, that's when we're at our most powerful. It takes a tremendous amount of inner strength to truly release our desire to control the people in our lives.

And whether we realize it or not, we *do* want to be in control. In fact, it's a prerequisite to adulthood. To be a functioning adult is to be responsible for your own welfare. Living a successful life requires you to become the master of your own fate—but it also requires you to release the illusion that you're the master of anyone else's.

MEET YOUR GRACIOUS SELF

The power and peace of acceptance is actualized through the development of what I call a Gracious Self. Your Gracious Self embraces the opportunity to recognize that everyone and everything in your life is a gift. It's acknowledging that when we consciously shift our focus to appreciate and accept our loved ones, happiness can readily replace noise in every circumstance and relationship.

Does acceptance erase or reverse all the relationship baggage we've accumulated over the years? No. But it does allow us to shift our focus away from the noise in our relationships and toward the good—the parts that feed our happiness. As Helen Keller once said, "Everything has its wonders, even darkness and silence, and I learn, whatever state I may be in, therein to be content." Acceptance is learning to be content, even in the dimmest of circumstances.

But before we can truly accept our loved ones, we have to stop judging them. Often, when we judge our loved ones, it's because we unconsciously see them as a reflection—or even a judgment—of ourselves. When a loved one brings out the best in us, we see that as proof that, underneath it all, we really are a great person, perfectly capable of getting along with anyone. But when they bring out the worst in us, we're slow to take credit for our own noisy behavior and reactions and quick to point a finger at someone else. No one likes to be reminded of their own impatience, short fuse, or passive-aggressive tendencies—and it's often those who are closest to us who bring those qualities to the surface.

When we have a history with someone, we carry the weight of the past into every interaction. And because humans have a negativity bias, we're more likely to recall the bad than the good. Acceptance asks us to acknowledge all of it—the good, the bad, and the ugly—but to dwell on the good. It asks us to approach our relationships with an appreciation for the value each person and moment adds to our lives, not with a mental laundry list of accumulated disappointments. It's natural for relationships to have both, but the one we feed is the one that grows.

WHAT ACCEPTANCE ISN'T

Acceptance isn't naive. Your Gracious Self is the part of you that approaches your relationships with gratitude and empathy, but also with nuance. Acceptance doesn't mean accepting the unacceptable. It doesn't mean "settling for less," "tolerating," "capitulating," or "surrendering." It's the exact opposite: acceptance empowers you. When you choose what to pay attention to—when you choose to be proactive rather than reactive—you're building the muscles you need to face anything life throws your way.

Acceptance isn't a quick fix. Acceptance requires an honest accounting and understanding of who you are, as well as how your loved ones have shaped and influenced you. It's not a magic wand that banishes all noise from your environment; it's an ongoing practice that enables you to choose happiness over noise—but you still have to make the choice.

Acceptance isn't easy. In order to accept, we have to be aware. Acceptance may mean challenging long-standing perceptions of our loved ones—not to mention ourselves.

Because we're attracted to what we know, we often don't recognize when a loved one or relationship is noisy. We become so entrenched in our long-standing relationship patterns that we take for granted how they affect us. To us, the nagging, subtle put-downs and guilting aren't issues; they're just part of the relationship dynamic. It often takes a neutral third party to see what we can't, helping us to become conscious of the noise in our relationships so that we might effectively block it.

Take the story of Laura and Ralph. A few years ago, Laura and her husband, Ralph, went to parent-teacher night at their son's school, where they met with his fourth-grade teacher. It was a tense half hour as the three of them discussed some recent behavioral issues their son was having.

At the end of the meeting, Ralph excused himself to go to the restroom and the teacher pulled Laura aside. She was concerned about the bickering and passive-aggressiveness she'd witnessed between the couple throughout the meeting; it was the exact pattern their son had been replicating in the classroom.

In that moment, Laura simply blushed and thanked the teacher for her concern. She then defensively recounted the conversation to Ralph on the ride home, trying to unite them against a common enemy. It was all "Who does she think she is?" and jokes about the fights their own parents used to have. That is, until Ralph forgot to stop at Costco, as Laura had requested. Suddenly they were back at it—and just like that, Laura realized that maybe the teacher had a point. At Laura's insistence, the couple began learning about nonviolent communication and eventually nipped the bickering in the bud.

But it wasn't an easy road. Even once she'd accepted the truth about how she and Ralph were communicating (that is, not well), Laura was still deeply ashamed that a practical stranger had insight into her marriage that she herself lacked. However, it's perfectly normal—even expected—that we become habituated to relationship noise. That's because the noise we're most susceptible to has likely been with us for far longer than any one relationship.

We often underestimate the impact our childhood and adolescent relationships can have on our adult lives. The fact is, most of us learn what's "normal" very early on and never question it again. Once her initial shock wore off, Laura was quickly able to realize that she had learned to bicker from her own parents, whose airing of petty grievances was part of the package they called "love." Ralph had a similar origin story. Together, they worked to find new ways of communicating love to each other.

Sometimes we have to look back to move forward

Understanding that they were both unintentionally bringing vintage noise into the relationship, they gave acceptance a shot. Instead of going tit for tat at the first sign of disagreement, they now call upon their Gracious Selves in times of conflict, and even just annoyance: "I recognize your noise. I understand your noise. I do not judge your noise. Our relationship is not defined by noise. I will love you in spite of your noise."

Acceptance isn't one-and-done. As they reinvented their relationship, Laura noticed that the resentment and anger she'd been feeling toward Ralph was starting to melt away. She felt lighter, happier . . . until she visited her mother, Mona, for a few days. Suddenly all that anger came rushing to the surface, shocking them both. Laura was upset that she'd wasted years of her life fighting with her husband, blaming it on her mother's example, while Mona—who'd always been revered by her daughter—protested that she could remember nothing but the love between herself and her late husband.

Laura had learned to block the noise in her marriage, but she forgot to extend her acceptance practice to her mother. It's a common oversight, really. When we have a relationship that's in need of repair, it usually doesn't prompt us to revamp how we show up in all of our relationships. That would be time-consuming, not to mention emotionally grueling! Luckily, acceptance doesn't require that we have hard confrontations with everyone in our lives. By changing our own responses to our loved ones—by accepting them and their noise—we also change how we show up in our relationships.

So how could Laura address this situation with her mom? She can engage in what I call the CHAIN OF GRATITUDE.

CHAIN OF GRATITUDE STEPS

The first link in the chain is ACCEPTANCE. Laura can recognize that she isn't responsible for her parents' noise. Even if she had been at the center of 99 percent of their arguments, that still wouldn't mean she had caused them—it was a choice they made. She's also not in charge of "punishing" Mona for the past, or forcing her to rewrite her personal understanding of what happened. If Laura can't heal or move forward until Mona accepts her version of things, she'll be waiting forever. Laura has to accept that Mona is still the woman she's idolized her whole life, and she's also a flawed human being with her own perspective on her marriage and her past.

The next link is EMPATHY. Laura knows firsthand that parenting is a nonstop exercise in humility. After all, she was entirely unaware that what she and Ralph considered "playful banter" was having a negative impact on her son—and it took a neutral third party, his teacher, to point it out. Did Laura's parents normalize that behavior when she was growing up? Sure. But maybe Mona got it from *her* parents—and on and on. The blame game could continue forever, or instead Laura could recognize how easy it is to fall into unhealthy patterns without even knowing it. And because she understands that her mother's noise is not her fault or responsibility—because she's accepted it—she's now positioned to empathize with her.

The third link in the Chain of Gratitude is (you guessed it) GRATITUDE. Now that Laura has accepted her mother as she is, and even empathized with her noise, she can choose to focus on all the positive aspects of their relationship. For example, Mona taught Laura that girls and women can break free from the social scripts they inherit. She encouraged her daughter to play in the dirt, to join Mathletes, to not rush into marriage or motherhood just because it was what others expected. For that alone, Laura has always been grateful—she just temporarily lost sight of the gifts of this relationship with her mom.

To be sure, some of us are not so lucky. Our familial relationships can range from healthy to toxic, but one thing they always are is influential—for better or worse. When we get off to a rough start, when our parents' noise results in neglect, addiction, or even abuse, it becomes difficult to find gratitude for the relationship. First, know how common it is, sadly, for a parent to betray their child. That's not to say it's okay, but it is to say that you're not alone—and you don't have to live your life in the shadow of someone else's noise. Second, all you have to do is understand your parents' noisy behavior and accept that it's not your responsibility. You don't have to condone it—or them. If nothing else, you can simply be grateful to your parents for the gift of life. For the ability to discover yourself, to fall in love, to have adventures, to see the world, to become a parent yourself.

Focus on the beauty you get to experience each day, all because someone gave birth to you.

Let's return to your hypothetical cat-lady aunt for a lighter example. Her constant commentary on your parenting choices drives you up a wall. Yet the thoughtful gifts she sends your children on holidays and birthdays shows that, on some level, she cares. She cares enough to remember important dates and to think of your family, even if you see each other once a year.

The delivery of her unsolicited parenting advice may be noisy, but there's an underlying sense of love and care beneath it all. Accept that you can't change her. Empathize with why she is the way she is: Did her sudden focus on your family start after her early retirement? Did she adopt all those cats because she had no outlet for her nurturing instincts? Is she lonely? Rather than focus on what she does wrong, find gratitude for what she does right.

Being truly grateful for the noisy people in our lives can be a downright magnificent experience. Despite the noise, you have come to recognize that some part of your interaction made you the wonderful person you are today. This is what it means to see the value in everyone and everything.

We've all got residual noise from childhood. It's easy to get angry at or run away from the people who created it. Acceptance is much harder, but it's worth it. Because the truth is, your acceptance isn't for those noisy folks; it's for you. Whether you see your mother every day or you haven't spoken in years, you'll live with the echoes of her noise until you make peace with yourself. How? By taking the perspective that every experience, person, emotion, and setback is a chance for you to grow, to move closer to your best self. No mistakes, no regrets—just growth opportunities.

Again, this is what it means to find the value in everything and everyone. If you recognize that all that noise had a purpose—to guide you toward your most powerful, authentic self—you can be grateful for it. You can be thankful for every aspect of who you are, warts and all. You know there's nothing to be ashamed of, no missteps that took you away from where you were meant to be. Instead of reliving your noise and regretting it, you say, "I went through that for a reason. I learned a lot about myself. I've grown, and now I'm bringing a better self into my next chapter."

PRACTICING ACCEPTANCE

Acceptance is not something you do once. It's an active part of your journey. I've found it helps to have mantras to repeat as you navigate the noise in your life. Here are five acceptance-themed mantras to get you started.

Acceptance Mantra No. 1: **"Let go and let God."**

As I said earlier, I love this mantra. "Let go and let God" is understanding that you're not responsible for anyone else's noise, nor can you change it.

Max out this mantra:

- I find myself reflecting on this one when people in my life are facing difficult hardships. Like many of us, I don't like to see my loved ones suffering. "Let go and let God" is a reminder that making someone else's suffering my responsibility won't change anything for them; it'll only result in both of us suffering.

- "Let go and let God" is a good reminder that we don't have divine powers, and we can't heal anyone but ourselves. We don't have the power to stop our loved one's suffering—only the power to choose whether we'll suffer along with them.

Acceptance Mantra No. 2: **"I will have the courage to experience the beauty of life."**

It's so common to feel guilty about being happy when our loved ones aren't. If they're a glass-half-empty kind of person, it's incredibly challenging for them to see it any other way. It's so important to accept that part of our loved one, *without allowing it to define who we are in the relationship.* Rather than criticize them for their negative views or wait for them to change their perspective, consider all that life has to offer you, and how you can take full advantage of it.

Max out this mantra:

- Start each day encouraged, energized, and excited to enjoy all that life has to offer. Each day is truly a gift that is ours to unwrap.

- All too often, we wait for someone else to take the initiative in our relationships—to plan a fun date, invite us out to a movie, or check out that new museum exhibit—all while taking little or no responsibility for our own role in the relationship. Be the one with the plan! Take yourself on a date, to a show, or on a leisurely walk. Whether you're creating opportunities to bond with your partner, your family, your friends, or just yourself, know that life is yours for the taking.

Acceptance Mantra No. 3: **"It's not that deep."**

In relationships, there are endless opportunities to make a mountain out of a molehill. This mantra is perfect when we need to take a step back and consider what's really worth fighting for.

Max out this mantra:

- Is it really that important if he doesn't put away his socks, or she doesn't organize her desk? Consider what really matters in your relationship and let go of the rest.

- Don't let a disagreement in the morning ruin your entire day. Disagreements are a part of relationships; they happen. Don't allow one to prevent you from enjoying the beauty of the day.

Acceptance Mantra No. 4: **"Think before you speak."**

If your partner does something that upsets you, how do you tend to approach them? Do you allow your frustration with them to justify doing things you know will upset them? Instead of acting out, pause and consider whether it's worth a discussion with your partner—and if it is, consider how and when.

Max out this mantra:

- Don't take everything to heart. The next time your feelings are hurt, take a moment to consider what it is you're really upset about. Many times, we'll find we're hurt not by what our partner did or said, but by what it brought up in us. In these moments, our reactions are opportunities for self-discovery and self-care.

- Remember: you are responsible for your own noise and happiness. Think about who you are in the relationship, and what you need from it. Are your needs realistic? Can you get what you need without trying to control your partner's noise? Is it your partner's noise that's the problem, or is it yours?

- Remember to pause and breath. Often we feel compelled to reply without giving ourselves the grace of self-reflection.

Acceptance Mantra No. 5: **"True happiness doesn't happen overnight."**

Relationships are one of life's greatest gifts and challenges. Remember to take the time to understand who your partner is, why you chose them, and how you relate to them.

Max out this mantra:

- Every relationship has noise. It's the type of noise—and how you handle it—that matters. How does the noise affect you? How does it compare with the happiness the relationship provides?

- Healthy and happy relationships take work. They are a process of self-discovery. Take time to understand what is important for you to lead a happy life.

> "YOU CAN'T HOLD A MAN DOWN WITHOUT STAYING DOWN WITH HIM."
> —BOOKER T. WASHINGTON

CHAPTER 5
FORGIVENESS AND LETTING GO

Forgiveness is an incredible phenomenon. Research suggests that it has substantial benefits for both forgiver and forgivee. Not only does it improve relationships, but it also decreases feelings of anxiety, depression, and anger while increasing feelings of hopefulness and self-esteem. It even boosts our immune system, decreases headaches, and lowers our blood pressure.

I know the power of forgiveness firsthand. It was forgiveness that ultimately enabled me to break free from the impact that my past traumatic experiences had on my life. Once I was able to forgive, I felt lighter, walked taller, and began to see the world through a completely different lens.

Sounds pretty great, right? So why do so many of us refuse to do it?

There are many reasons why we withhold forgiveness. We don't want to forget, so we refuse to forgive. Many of us hold the unspoken belief that to forgive is to be naive, that forgiveness means we haven't learned anything from a betrayal.

It's also far easier to hold on to our bitter feelings than it is to forgive. There's a sense of power that comes with holding a grudge or standing your ground. However, that power is a mirage. Far more powerful—and tougher—is letting go of the noise. I often remind myself of what Booker T. Washington once said: "You can't hold a man down without staying down with him."

Let's look at some of the things we say to justify why we're withholding forgiveness:

> **Forgiveness Roadblocks**
> - *I was right.*
> - *I never received an apology.*
> - *We're not on speaking terms anyway.*
> - *I'm not ready.*
> - *I can't forget.*
> - *Some things are unforgivable.*

Reading that list can be a bit of a gut punch, simply because so many of us have said or felt these things before. There's a gravity to each of these emotional statements, and because we can all relate to them, they're easy to defend.

But perhaps they're so relatable that, when we hear them or say them, we take them at face value without prodding deeper. When that happens, these expressions stop describing legitimate feelings and start sounding a whole lot like unprocessed noise. Take the first point: let's assume that you were—and are—right. Does that make holding a grudge and losing a relationship any less painful? An adage comes to mind: do you want to be right, or do you want to be happy?

One thing we must realize is that forgiveness isn't really about the person you're forgiving. It's about you. You're not letting go of anger and resentment to validate or absolve anyone's actions. You're letting go because anger and resentment are detrimental to your own happiness.

FORGIVING YOURSELF

More often than not, the person we really need to forgive is ourselves. It can be difficult to let go of the things we've done. We start playing a never-ending game of *If only I'd done this, if only I'd said that, if only—*

Stop right there. Remember: there are no mistakes, only opportunities to grow. Are you seizing them, or are you dwelling on things that no one—not even you—can change?

Right here, right now, forgive yourself for . . .

- Not being able to handle a loved one's noise 24/7. Some people are so noisy that we can interact with them only in small doses, or when the stakes are low. Just because you're able to feel grateful for your cat-lady aunt doesn't mean you now have to invite her on every intimate family vacation from here on out.

- Not being ready to share physical space with a noisy loved one. You can accept someone's noise, empathize with them, be grateful for the relationship, and even forgive them—but still not be ready to interact beyond that. And that's okay! While you might eventually be prepared to face them, today's not that day. So be it. Forgiveness is saying, "I accept you for who you are. I don't hold any grudges or harbor any resentment. I'm not holding on to noise." It doesn't require that you invite them back into your life.

- Hoping you don't run into them. Were you secretly crossing your fingers that a *Golden Girls* marathon would keep Cat Auntie home from the family reunion? Not only is that okay; it's totally normal. Just because we've accepted the noisy people in our lives doesn't mean we can't hope for a peaceful afternoon with our favorite noise-free people.

forgiveness is the greatest gift

EXERCISE: PRACTICING FORGIVENESS

Think of the following exercise as a dry run for forgiveness. The idea is to have a practice to help you untangle resentment, anger, guilt, and other feelings standing between you and your happiness. This practice is just for you—you don't have to engage anyone else to reap the benefits.

1 **STEP 1:** Pick one person you need to forgive, or a person you desire forgiveness from. You can choose yourself, a person you've lost track of, or even a deceased loved one—again, this practice is for you and does not require communication with anyone else.

2 **STEP 2:** List three reasons you need to forgive or be forgiven by this person.

3 **STEP 3:** List three ways withholding your forgiveness or having forgiveness withheld from you has impacted your life.

4 **STEP 4:** List three ways you would feel if you forgave or were forgiven.

_____

_____

_____

5 **STEP 5:** Complete the sentence that makes sense for your situation:

I forgive _____ for _____.

I am forgiven for

_____.

6 **STEP 6:** Experience forgiveness by reading your sentence out loud. Repeat this practice as often and with as many scenarios as you need to.

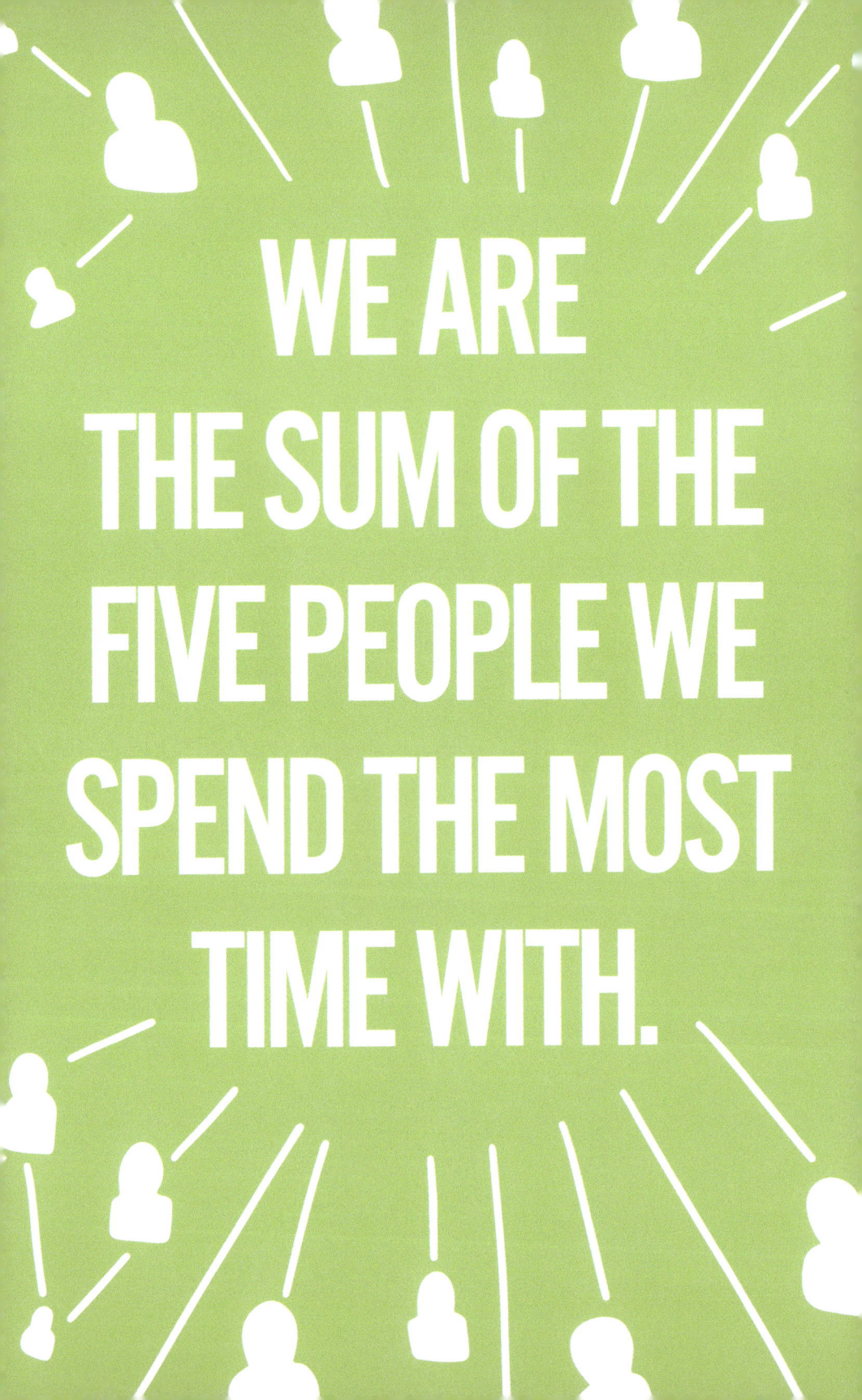

WE ARE THE SUM OF THE FIVE PEOPLE WE SPEND THE MOST TIME WITH.

CHAPTER 6
ASSEMBLING YOUR A-TEAM

It has been said that we are all the sum of the five people we spend the most time with.

How does that idea make you feel? Your gut reaction is telling: Did you nod along and smile at the thought of your five ride-or-dies? Did your stomach sink as you realized that your relationships have been on autopilot, tailored for convenience rather than nourishment? Or are you currently reckoning with the fact that you can think of only three people you spend time with—and you claim two of them on your taxes?

For most of us, it takes a lot more than five people to reflect everything we are. Yet the older and busier we become, the harder it is to maintain, let alone expand, our social circle. Instead, we turn to our partners or children to fulfill most, if not all, of our social needs. After years of this, we end up neglecting or even forgetting the aspects of ourselves that aren't compatible with our daily grind. We forget all the color and joy our other relationships used to provide. This chapter is devoted to remembering, celebrating, and appreciating *all* of our special relationships—the ones we have with our A-Team.

Who is your A-Team? It's anyone and everyone who inspires you, supports you, or otherwise enhances your life. It's your partner and kids (hopefully), but it's also that friend you have a million and one inside jokes with, the one who cracks you up like no other. It's the trustworthy friend you share your deepest, darkest secrets with, and the industry friend who is generous with her connections and has the best career advice. It's the acquaintance who loves mountain biking, karaoke, or game night just as much as you do, and the woman from your Mommy and Me group whose laid-back attitude makes you feel like you just took a meditation class. It's the ex you remained friends with after the breakup, the one who taught you that a relationship doesn't have to end if it can evolve. It's that old co-worker you still grab lunch with every quarter to unpack the latest industry gossip, and the generous neighbor who always hooks you up with her delicious family recipes and an invite to the barbecue.

When it comes to our A-Team, quality trumps quantity. You might not see or talk to these folks all that often, but when you do, it's always time well spent. These are the people who reflect to you how complex, deep, and rich your life really is.

Nurturing these relationships doesn't just feed our souls; it improves our other relationships, too. When we rely on one person—typically our partner—to be our plus-one for every yard sale, concert, and Saturday morning hike, we're putting undue stress on our relationship.

THE MVP OF YOUR A-TEAM

From a young age, we're taught to find not just a partner, but a soulmate. Someone who completes us in every way, and vice versa. I feel very fortunate to have married my best friend. Now, before you roll your eyes (no judgment—I would too), it's not unicorns and rainbows all day, every day. Marriage takes work, and part of that work is nourishing what you enjoy about each other, not attempting to change the other person. While my husband is truly my number one, I know he doesn't share my profound appreciation for reality TV—and he understands that I will never know (or care) which college football teams make up the Big Ten.

If happiness requires us to embrace all the things that make us who we are, a loving relationship should never require us to replace our personal passions with compromises. Instead of requiring our partner to tag along for all of our adventures—even the ones they have no interest in—we can simply enjoy ourselves with a friend who'd love nothing more than to spend her Saturday haggling with retirees at a yard sale or hitting the hiking trail. Instead of harming one of our most significant relationships by being overreliant on it, we can bolster two relationships at the same time—not to mention the relationship we have with ourselves.

Regardless of the role a person plays in our lives, we should always strive to be aware of the stress we're putting on a given relationship. Relying on a friend to meet all of our needs is no better than relying on a partner, a child, or anyone else. I'm my own cautionary tale when it comes to this. I'm a naturally shy person, so when I first began building my A-Team, I had a tendency to gravitate toward one person. They weren't just my best friend, they were my everything: my champion, my muse, my shoulder to cry on . . . anything and everything under the sun.

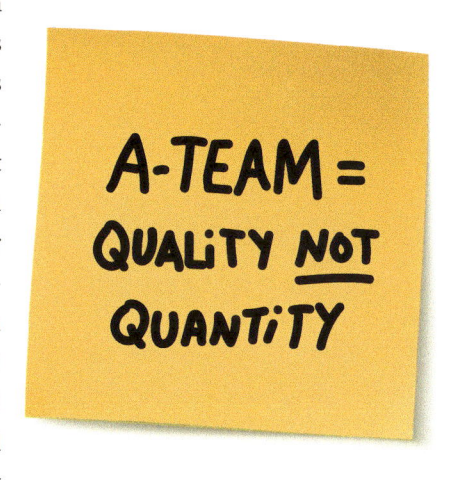

Of course, this approach was destined to fail. Once you assign every role or responsibility to one person, they're bound to disappoint you—simply because what you're expecting of them is impossible. No one can be someone's everything. As difficult and scary as it can be to put ourselves out there, having a well-balanced A-Team ensures that we avoid hurting the people we love with unrealistic expectations.

BUILDING YOUR BENCH WITH CARE

Just as we can't expect one person to carry our entire team, we also don't want to pad our team with a bunch of random people in the hope that they'll magically fill our gaps. Building an A-Team is an ongoing process that requires us to be thoughtful—and patient. Meaningful relationships don't form overnight, or by force: we have to cultivate them and see how they blossom before determining they are the right fit. In other words, we don't want to "assign" people to our A-Team because we think they suit a particular role; we want to include them because they take on that role autonomously and organically.

While we all know when a relationship or friendship "feels right," we may have a harder time determining our compatibility with people we have transactional relationships with, people like therapists, coaches, physical trainers, or spiritual teachers. We may think our tendency to clam up at the therapist's office is just a normal, uncomfortable part of the process, or that a spiritual leader explaining away our intuitions is just more "enlightened" than we are—they must know better than we do, right?

The truth is, it takes a lot of trial, error, and effort to find the right people to journey with. It's just like a romantic relationship: you're not going to click with any ol' therapist. You'll probably have to "date around" before finding someone who feels right. And there will be someone out there who feels right—it might just take time to find them. If someone doesn't pass your vibe check, it doesn't mean you've failed—it just means you're not done auditioning people for that role yet. Building an A-Team is building a support system—*your* support system. No one deserves a spot on your roster simply because they're willing and able.

Now, let's assemble your A-Team!

EXERCISE: A-TEAM, ASSEMBLE!

Remember the superlatives from your high school yearbook? Students would vote to recognize their most exceptional classmates across all kinds of categories, from Best Hair to Most Likely to Succeed. Now it's your turn to present all the awards to your best and brightest—your A-Team.

But first, a few guidelines before you get started:

Your A-Team should include anyone who plays a generative role in your life, no matter how big or small it is. That includes everyone from your partner and kids to that one friend you always fall into easy conversation with, no matter how much time has passed. Anyone you've shared a special connection with—even if it's currently inactive—should be considered.

You can award the same person with multiple titles, and you can award the same title to multiple people. However, if someone is playing more than three roles for you, you should reflect on your expectations of them, and of the relationship—especially if those roles are on the emotionally taxing side.

Now, without further ado, let's build your A-Team!

1 **STEP 1:** Open a fresh page in your journal and start brainstorming. As you read this chapter, what faces and names popped into your mind? A longtime mentor? A life coach? A reliable neighbor? Your BFF from sleepaway camp? Jot down the names of anyone you'd consider part of your A-Team. Feel free to include any key words about the role they play in your life.

2 **STEP 2:** On a fresh page, write down as many of your relationship needs as you can think of. What activities do you need or want a partner for? What kind of support—and release—do you need? Your needs can be emotional (*I need to feel it's safe to be vulnerable; I need to laugh*), interest-based (*I need a rock-climbing partner; I need someone to enjoy live music with*), physical (*I need hugs; I need* someone to share household responsibilities with), goal-oriented (*I need someone who will give me feedback on my writing; I need someone who can help me understand personal finance*), or related to connection (*I need someone to tell me the truth; I need someone I can talk to for hours*).

3 **STEP 3**: Return to your list of names from step 1. Do any of them meet the needs you listed in step 2? Mark that down. If a name on your list doesn't correspond to any of the needs you wrote down, dig deeper. Why did you include this person on your A-Team? What need do they fulfill that you may have overlooked during the last step? Add it to your list.

4 **STEP 4**: Now that you have an idea of the roles your A-Team plays for you, it's time to recognize them for all the value they add to your life. Working down your list of relationship needs, translate each one into a superlative on a fresh page, leaving a few lines of space below each one. For example, "I need someone to enjoy live music with" becomes "Most Likely to Take My Extra Concert Ticket, No Questions Asked." Have fun with it!

Here are a few superlatives from my life to help get you started:

- Most Likely to Make Me Laugh About Nothing
- Most Likely to Drive Me to the Emergency Room in the Middle of the Night
- Most Likely to Dominate the Dance Floor with Me
- Most Likely to Keep My Secrets
- Most Likely to Feed My Soul
- Most Likely to Recommend My Next Favorite Book, Musician, or Artist
- Most Likely to Tell Me the Truth When I Don't Want to Hear It
- Most Likely to Ignite My Inner Child

- Most Likely to Spend Hours Helping Me Find the Perfect Outfit
- Most Likely to Help Me Move
- Most Likely to Be My Mentor
- Most Likely to Support My Creative Endeavors
- Most Likely to Inspire Me
- Most Likely to Listen Without Judgment
- Most Likely to Celebrate My Wins Like They're Her Own
- Most Likely to Catch a Last-Minute Movie with Me
- Most Likely to Join Me on Vacation
- Most Likely to Encourage My Dreams

STEP 5: Once you have your list of superlatives, write down the names from step 1 that correspond to each award. Reflect:

• Are there any superlatives with no names under them? Maybe you have a lot of emotionally supportive members of your A-Team but none who know how to cut back and relax. Be aware of any needs you've listed that aren't being fulfilled—that means there's room in your life for new connections.

• Is there anyone playing more than three roles? Pay special attention to the health of these connections, and whether you may be overreliant on them. If you are, decide which of their roles are most unique and important, and whether you can meet the remaining needs with other relationships.

• Are there people you've fallen out of touch with on your A-Team? With a new understanding of how much you value them, there's no better time to reconnect.

6 **STEP 6:** For extra credit, take the same list of superlatives and change "Most Likely" to "Least Likely." Assign each of these to someone on your A-Team. After all, the point of building an A-Team is not just to help us recognize all the relationships that enhance our lives—it's also to help us recognize that one person cannot be responsible for everything. The person you have the most fun with might not be the first person you call in an emergency, and that's perfectly okay! By doing this exercise in reverse, you'll have a better understanding of the gifts and limitations of each member of your A-Team. This will keep your expectations realistic and your relationships healthy.

Now, pat yourself on the back for cultivating a life full of dynamic people and relationships! And not to worry if there are still a few gaps to fill. Your A-Team—like all of your relationships—is a work in progress. Seek support where you find it lacking, and appreciate all the love you already have.

YOUR A-TEAM	RELATIONSHIP NEEDS

SUPERLATIVES	MATCHING A-TEAM MEMBERS
Most Likely to Make Me Laugh →	*Jimmy, Julia*

THE ROAD TO HAPPINESS IS ONE OF SELF-DISCOVERY.

CHAPTER 7
INTRODUCING YOURSELF TO ... YOURSELF

Now that we've shone a light on who you are in relationships, it's time to gain a deeper understanding of yourself.

Who are you?

Think about it for a moment. When you try to answer that question, what first comes to mind?

Is it your soul?

Is it your personality?

Is it your behavior?

Is it your accomplishments?

Is it your mistakes?

Is it the sum of your experiences?

Is it inside?

Is it outside?

Is it all of the above? None of the above?

For me, the answer is some complicated mix of all of the above. What comes to mind for you? Who you are—who each of us is—is intricate and nuanced. As a result, what makes you happy will have a unique, ornate pattern to it. It's like a fingerprint: it belongs to you and you alone. What works for us won't work for others, and vice versa—which is why the road to happiness is one of self-discovery. You really can't have one without the other.

The goal of self-discovery is to meet and understand your Complete Self. To get there, we first have to become acquainted with our Public Self and our Private Self.

MEET YOUR PUBLIC SELF

All of us have a Public Self. This is the part of us that participates in social dynamics, the part we share with the world. It's who we are at work or school, and with family, friends, and acquaintances. It's both our social media presence and how we interact with the cashier at the supermarket.

Most of us conduct ourselves differently in the public sphere than we do when we're at home or alone. From our mannerisms to our speech, we project the parts of ourselves that we want to share with others. Our Public Self is the part of us that's tailored to this kind of engagement. It helps us foster relationships, participate in our communities, and enrich the world around us.

Our Public Self has many manifestations. It embodies who we are with friends, but also who we are at work, on social media, and while sitting in the middle seat of an airplane. Our Public Self is a bit of a chameleon, adapting to the different environments, people, and circumstances we encounter. It's a spectrum of our attributes, behaviors, beliefs, and experiences that come to light depending on the context we're in. That doesn't mean our Public Self is a fake self, though—it's a genuine part of who we are.

Take work, for example. Regardless of our personal style, there's typically a part of our wardrobe that's reserved for work-appropriate attire—whether that's a uniform, a suit and tie, or an apron. While at work, most of our conversations will revolve around what we're there to do, and likewise, we'll follow the etiquette and cultural expectations of our workplace. Our co-workers may know about our interests outside of work, but we're not going to give a presentation on the sourdough bread we baked last weekend or ask for a raise based on our hula-hooping skills. At the end of the day, we're at work to play a specific role. Playing that role doesn't change anything about who we are. We're simply shining a light on the aspects of our personality that are appropriate for that role.

OUR SOCIAL MEDIA SELF

One permutation of the Public Self that demands special consideration is the role we play on social media. In many ways, social media allows us to construct our ideal Public Self. Think of those modern Norman Rockwell images we see so often on Instagram: Mom, Dad, Son, and Daughter are beaming from ear to ear in front of the crystal blue ocean, just as the sun sets below the horizon. Their outfits are impeccable—not a wrinkle or stain in sight. They're practically welcoming you to join them in paradise.

Here's what you don't see in that photo: It took forty-five minutes and three strangers to capture a shot where the kids weren't pulling each other's hair and sand wasn't blowing into Dad's eye. The wrinkle-free outfits were bought brand-new after wandering the mall for two hours because the airline lost everyone's luggage. That sparkling blue water? It's a filter. What isn't these days?

So is it a lie? We may be tempted to think so—many of us struggle with the chasm between who we are "in real life" and who we are online. But the truth is, there's nothing fraudulent about presenting an edited version of ourselves online (unless you're Facetuning your arms out of existence). Even if you spend hours writing captions and auditioning different filters, it's still you who's deciding which aspects of yourself to project. All of us have a best foot to put forward, an aspirational version of ourselves we're working toward. What we aspire to be is as much a part of us as anything else.

Of course, there does come a point where our filtered photos create more noise than happiness. It's in those instances when the photo doesn't represent our best or aspirational self, but a false self, a lie, an attempt to hide who we truly are.

Say the beaming couple in the beautiful post is actually on the verge of divorce. While their vacation pic may assure the viewers at home that they've never been more in love, no filter on earth can mask the truth for the people living it: the marriage is on its way to over. Still, they post the pretty photo anyway—if not to convince others, then maybe to convince themselves.

This is not the same thing as posting a picture that took several takes and a bit of begging and pleading to pull off. This is projecting aspects of ourselves that don't hold true to who we are or who we hope to become. We can edit a photo so that it expresses what's truly inside of us, but we can't edit the emotional truth of a situation. When we put on a happy front by posting a photo like this, all the #couplegoals comments in the world will only serve as a stark reminder of the harsh reality. A Public Self rooted in disingenuousness will create noise—no matter how many likes we garner in the process.

What's most important is that we're able to be honest with ourselves. Our children will not always be perfect, our skin will not always be flawless, and our vacations will not always be epic. That doesn't mean we have to post all the outtakes from our family photo shoots to be authentic. Remember: your edited photos are just as much of a reflection of who you are as any candid. Just make sure that when you edit your photos, it's not an attempt to hide the truth but to project it—to reflect the beauty you see in yourself and your loved ones. There's nothing more real than that.

MEET YOUR PRIVATE SELF

Life is always unfolding, even in the moments when no one else is around. These quiet moments belong to the Private Self. This is who you are at home, with headphones on during the commute, walking down the street, or jogging on the treadmill. This is who you are when practicing your half of a conversation in the shower or accepting an award in the mirror. It's who you are when you're alone with your thoughts.

The Private Self is the part of us that's for us alone. It's the part we don't necessarily share with others. It's the stream of consciousness that narrates our joys, hardships, experiences, and desires. Your Private Self speaks loudly about your likes, dislikes, and everything in between. It's the part of us that is autonomous and unfiltered, the quiet conversation we have in our mind as we go through the day, reaffirming what we believe to be true.

Whether the conversation in our head feeds our happiness or creates noise is crucial. Our Private Self is not more "true," "authentic," or "real" than our Public Self, but it can be noisier. When we voice negative or potentially harmful beliefs out loud, we're likely to get feedback that at least makes us pause and question what we think. Hidden away within us, our Private Self is far less subject to outside intervention. Without a neutral third party to reflect our Private Self back to us, we're at risk of fostering noisy beliefs and depleting our happiness.

We all have an internal dialogue, an ongoing conversation that takes place in our mind. Some of those conversations are noisier than others. For example, we all know how it feels at that perfect moment when our intellect and instinct align and we know, without a doubt, what the right next step is. We know exactly what to do, how to do it, and where we need to be to make it happen. But the decision-making process is often not that straightforward. Sometimes our inner dialogue is a push-and-pull about what to do next. We debate every decision and potential next move, entering a seemingly endless deliberation as we predict and ponder what could happen. The longer this goes on, the noisier things get. What we need when this happens is distance from our own thoughts. One way to gain this distance and clarity is by journaling all the thoughts and images running through our mind, giving form to some of our anxieties and making them easier to tackle one by one. When we take our ruminations out of our head and put them on paper, we're better equipped to consider them from an objective perspective. We can see more easily which considerations are valid, and which aren't worth dwelling on.

We also use our inner voice to rehearse what we'll say in situations before they happen, hosting a two-way conversation in our head to prep for the real thing. We run through our little monologues like lines in a play, over and over, until we have the opportunity to deliver them out loud. But as we prepare for our big scene, it's easy to lose sight of how we feel. The impulse to extensively prepare for such a conversation signals anxiety and doubt, which can manifest as feelings of sadness, inadequacy, confusion, and, of course, noise.

While these feelings are natural, they don't have to become all-consuming. It starts with noticing that we're having them, though. When you find yourself rehearsing what to say over and over, pause and take a deep breath. Unless this conversation is a matter of life or death, it's simply not that deep. Don't allow the preparation and buildup to become worse than the actual event.

While the Private Self can be noisy, it also provides us with a kind of happiness we can't find anywhere else. Without the noise of the outside world, we're free to shine a light on who we really are. In public, we're expected to uphold certain standards and practices, some of which require us to wall off certain parts of ourselves. But our Private Self is free to think, feel, and behave naturally. It allows us to be introspective without societal boundaries or expectations, enabling us to feed and enrich all the amazing parts of who we are without judgment or fear.

It's when we're alone with our Private Self that we're most connected to our raw essence. Your Private Self is who you are when all the lights are off. It's who you are when you're connected to a higher power, whatever that means for you. It's who you are when you're in meditation or prayer. It allows every aspect of you to shine without obfuscation or filters. It's your inner monologue. It's your decision-making process. It's the internal push-and-pull that we all go through. It's your hopes, wishes, dreams, and fears. It's you—raw, unfiltered, and irreplaceable.

MEET YOUR COMPLETE SELF

Humans are social creatures. We can't survive in complete isolation. At the same time, if we're out twenty-four hours a day, we need moments to be introspective. To achieve balance, we need to be able to connect with ourselves *and* with others. This is our Complete Self: a harmonious blend of who we are in relationships and who we are when we're alone with our thoughts.

Your Complete Self is the person you enjoy being, regardless of who's watching. It knows your fears, desires, hopes, interests, dreams, abilities, achievements, and mistakes. Your Complete Self is your number one fan, best friend, and mentor, all in one. Its love, support, and guidance are unconditional and unwavering, as you discover every challenge and reward life has to offer. Your Complete Self is curious, courageous, and comfortable making mistakes; it is eager to learn and grow. It recognizes that today's mistakes are tomorrow's opportunities. It does not judge your feelings, behaviors, or experiences but rather appreciates and grows from them. Your Complete Self cherishes every aspect of the magnificent person you are.

EXERCISE: EXPLORING YOUR COMPLETE SELF

It's time to take what you've just read and make it personal. Getting specific will help you better understand your Complete Self.

1 **STEP 1:** First we'll explore your **PUBLIC SELF**. Open up to a fresh page in your journal and brainstorm the different "audiences" you engage with on a regular basis, as well as the places where you encounter them and the activities you partake in together. An audience can be one specific person or a group of people. Here are some common examples to get you started:

- My family, at home
- My co-workers, at the office
- My social media followers, on Instagram, etc.
- My partner, on a special occasion
- My book club, on Zoom
- My kids' friends' parents, at birthday parties
- My long-distance friend, catching up on the phone
- My industry peers, at a conference
- My vocal coach, during my singing lessons
- My students, while teaching class
- My hairdresser, at the salon
- My mother, on our weekly visits
- Strangers, while shopping for groceries

2 **STEP 2:** Making your way down your list, answer the following questions about the Public Self that presents itself based on the relationship and/or context.

- *How do you dress?*
- *What impression do you want to make?*
- *How do you think you're received?*
- *Are you funny or serious?*
- *Are you reserved or candid?*
- *Do you talk more or listen more?*
- *Are you more vulnerable or guarded, or do you feel free to speak and act authentically?*
- *What makes the interaction feel like a success? What makes it feel like a failure?*
- *How do you feel, think, and behave during the interaction?*
- *How do you feel, think, and behave after the interaction?*

Note the similarities and differences in how you present yourself to different people. You may notice that you interact with your mother the same way you would a particularly noisy friend, or that you have many intimate relationships where you give too much and receive too little. You may also notice that some relationships and contexts allow you to be your full, authentic self, or that your social media posts don't align with how you want to be seen. Make note of whatever comes up, and what improvements or shifts can be made.

STEP 1	**STEP 2**
Public Self audiences	*How do you engage?*

3 **STEP 3**: Now we're going to explore your **PRIVATE SELF**. Turn to a fresh page in your journal and create a chart with three columns.

In **COLUMN A**, list the things about you that feed your happiness. This can include your personality traits, talents or skills, behaviors, experiences, and aspirations. Don't worry about what other people would say about you if they were answering this question—all that matters for this step is your own opinion. It's okay if your answers would normally embarrass you—include all your out-of-the-box thoughts, wildest aspirations, and biggest dreams.

In **COLUMN B**, list the things about you that foster noise. What makes you doubt or question yourself? What makes you feel ashamed? What thoughts do you have about yourself that are guaranteed to rain on your parade or kill your buzz? Which of your actions have sent you spiraling, even if there were not external consequences attached?

In **COLUMN C**, list those attributes that fall in between—these are traits or beliefs that are sometimes happy, sometimes noisy. A strong belief in personal excellence might have you striving to be the best at everything you do, but it may also have you setting impossible standards for yourself. You may love nurturing people but struggle to honor their independence as a result.

4 **STEP 4**: Review your three columns. What themes do you notice? Was it easier to come up with happier attributes or noisier attributes? Can you use anything from your list in column A to balance or heal your list in column B? Write a page or two reflecting on your experience and addressing any patterns that emerged.

COLUMN A

What about you feeds happiness?

COLUMN B

What about you fosters noise?

COLUMN C

What about you is both?

A NOISY THOUGHT THROWS US INTO A SPIRAL OF SECOND-GUESSING OR DOUBTING OURSELVES.

CHAPTER 8
IDENTIFYING NOISY THOUGHTS

One of the greatest challenges I've faced as a mother—and there have been many—is figuring out how to get through each day without chipping away at my happiness. On any given day, a child may come home from a less-than-stellar day at school (middle school does not get easier), or I may spend a little too much time on a parenting website (there is such a thing as too much advice), or something will trigger an insecurity that rattles around in my thoughts all day (*Did anyone notice that my bake sale brownies came from Costco?*).

While noise is ever-present, it need not be all-powerful. I like to think of noise as being like the Wizard in *The Wizard of Oz*: once you pull back the curtain, à la Dorothy, you realize that what you thought was a threat is nothing more than an annoying menace.

Let's continue our work of pulling back the curtain on noise. In the last chapter, you developed an understanding of how noise interacts with your Private and Public Selves. Now we want to explore how that noise mangles our thoughts, experiences, and behaviors.

Thanks to many incredible researchers in the field of psychology, noisy thoughts have been given a lot of attention, and even have their own field: "cognitive distortions." Cognitive distortions are patterns in our thinking and behavior that are both inaccurate and psychologically damaging. Noisy thoughts often manifest as limiting beliefs about ourselves, which we use cherry-picked facts to support. They're stubborn and extreme, and they sound something like this:

- *I'm not good enough.*
- *Nothing ever works out for me.*
- *I knew that was going to happen.*
- *No one cares what I think.*
- *I feel it, so it must be true.*
- *I should have . . . / I shouldn't have . . .*
- *If only I'd . . .*

QUICK TIP *When you're unsure whether a thought is noise or a fact, ask yourself: would I say this to a trusted friend? If the answer is no, you can toss that thought in the noise bin and move on with your day.*

NOISY THOUGHTS: A CHEAT SHEET

While noisy thoughts can feel very specific and personal, most cognitive distortions belong to one of ten categories. Being able to categorize your noisy thoughts is like following your clothing's care instructions on laundry day: you can toss them all into the washer in one massive heap, but you'll get better results if you separate them and care for them according to specific instructions.

All-or-nothing thinking: These are thoughts that color your world in absolutes. Rather than a world of possibilities, you see two opposite extremes with no in-between.

Overgeneralization: This is when one flaw, failure, mistake, or negative experience becomes how you define yourself or an aspect of your life—for example, believing that a failed relationship means you're unworthy of love or meant to be alone forever.

Mental filtering: This is the tendency to ignore the positive and see only the negative.

Jumping to conclusions: This is the inaccurate belief that you know how a situation will end or what another person is thinking. It often involves assuming the worst, regardless of the facts.

Magnification and minimization: This is the tendency to emphasize or focus on the negatives while diminishing the importance or likelihood of the positives.

Emotional reasoning: This is when you give your feelings the status of fact, without accounting for the transient nature of emotions or any other factors beyond your present emotional state.

"Should" statements: This is when your thoughts are clouded with critical judgments that center on the words "should," "shouldn't," "must," "ought to," and "have to."

Labeling: This happens when you assign an overgeneralized label to yourself or others, based on one negative experience.

Fallacy of change: These thoughts come in two forms: external and internal. When they're external, you believe you have the ability to change someone else's feelings or behaviors. When they're internal, you believe that your life is beyond your control and there's nothing you can do to change it.

Personalization: This happens when you feel compelled to take responsibility for situations or issues that have nothing to do with you. You take the blame for events that are out of your control and impossible for you to influence.

Noisy thoughts are a challenge to our Complete Self, because they cloud our perception of who we really are and can blossom into doubt, anxiety, and depression. The cycle unfolds like this: First, something prompts us to question ourselves. It can be a situation that's unfolding in the present, a past experience, or even a fleeting thought as we go about our day. Regardless of its source, a noisy thought throws us into a spiral of second-guessing or doubting ourselves.

Next, we make a decision based on that thought. We might decide that, because we didn't get the job we wanted, we're not qualified to do anything that would make us happy. Instead of pursuing additional training or working to improve our interview skills, we start considering jobs that we're overqualified for. Or maybe we give up the search entirely, even though we can't actually afford to do so. We may even blame the organization or the interviewers, sending a scorched-earth email to let them know they blew it—and destroying any goodwill we may have garnered in the process.

Finally, we end up forgoing or avoiding future opportunities that would prove our noisy thoughts wrong. We don't seek the additional training we may need, so we stay stuck where we are. We don't ask for feedback, so we don't know which areas to improve. When we do this, we miss the chance to dispel the distortion. Rather than challenge the noisy thought, we reinforce it, lending it more and more credence until it becomes our reality.

The good news is that the earlier we're able to recognize and identify noisy thoughts, the better chance we have of breaking the cycle before it can take root.

Let's now dive deeper into each flavor of noisy thought. While we're all capable of having these thoughts from time to time, there are likely a few you've recognized as patterns in your own thinking. As you read, take note of which distortions you experience most often, and the circumstances or people that tend to trigger them.

You may also find it helpful to take notice of your loved ones falling into one of these mental traps. For example, because I'm always wearing my mom hat, I try to notice these thinking patterns popping up for my children when they share their experiences with me. When you identify cognitive distortions that your loved ones struggle with, make note of what you say, think, and feel when they're struggling. Recognizing cognitive distortions in others often helps us get more attuned to recognizing them in ourselves. You can refer back to these notes when you start slipping into your own noisy thoughts.

ALL-OR-NOTHING THINKING

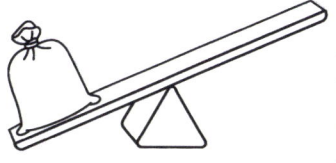

When all-or-nothing thoughts flood your mind, you can see only in black and white. No shades of gray, no color—it's either one extreme or the other. Rather than accept that life is complicated, we lose all sense of nuance: a situation or person is either totally horrible or absolutely perfect.

Let's say you approach a job interview with all-or-nothing thinking. In your mind, a job offer will validate everything about you: your education, your career choices, your people skills, and more. But if you don't get the job, you'll believe instead that you're a complete failure, as though everything you've done up until this moment was a waste of time. Either way, all of your self-worth is wrapped up in this process. You're unable to account for all the variables that go into the hiring process—either you get the job and you're awesome, or you don't get the job and you're a loser.

It's a pretty extreme position to take, but that's all-or-nothing thinking for you. There's no middle ground. There's no space to say, "I didn't get the job because they hired the recruiter's cousin," or "I didn't get the job because the other candidate's salary requirements were lower." You just believe you're a failure. That you lost and someone else won. You fail to recognize that life isn't a competition, that there's good to be found in the bad and bad to be found in the good. All-or-nothing thinking tricks you into reducing the messy and beautiful experience of living into absolutes that simply don't—and can't—exist.

> **Journal Prompts:**
> - *Where in my life do I tend to go to extremes?*
> - *How do I feel when my loved ones engage in all-or-nothing thinking? What do I say? What do I want to say?*
> - *What can I tell myself when I start to fall into all-or-nothing thinking?*

OVERGENERALIZATION

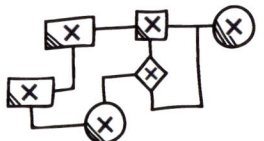

Overgeneralization is taking one flaw, failure, mistake, or negative experience and generously applying it to all unrelated future experiences.

Say you couldn't find your child in the grocery store for a few panic-stricken moments. Rather than treat it as a brief mishap to learn from, you base all of your future parenting decisions on not allowing it to happen again. You become overcautious and overbearing, responding to the world not as it is, but as your fears tell you it could be.

Not only are you now controlled by this distortion, but your growing child is also forced to abide by fears and rules that have no logical basis—and you won't allow them to prove otherwise by giving them opportunities to take developmentally appropriate risks.

Journal Prompts:

- *Which mistakes do I allow myself, and which do I go out of my way to avoid making again?*
- *How do I feel when my loved ones overgeneralize? What do I say? What do I want to say?*
- *What can I tell myself when I start to overgeneralize?*

MENTAL FILTERING

As humans, we all have a negativity bias. We not only notice negative stimuli more readily than positive stimuli; we also tend to dwell more on the negatives. In that sense, we're always engaged in some degree of mental filtering: our brains are like colanders, collecting all the negatives while the positives flow down the drain.

Let's say that after the experience at the grocery store, you come home and recount what happened to your partner. They reassure you that you're an incredible parent—in fact, people tell you so all the time. But your mind is still laser-focused on the grocery store. You find yourself filtering out the compliment and instead ruminating over what happened that afternoon, digesting the thought that you are a bad parent.

Journal Prompts:

- *What do I tend to focus on? Do I give criticism more weight than compliments? How quickly can I recount the compliments I've received recently?*

- *How seriously do I take compliments in general? Am I able to receive them and believe them? Do I compliment myself? Or am I my own worst critic?*

- *How do I feel when my loved ones engage in mental filtering? What do I say? What do I want to say?*

- *What can I tell myself when I start to fall into mental filtering?*

JUMPING TO CONCLUSIONS

When we jump to conclusions, we make negative assumptions or determinations without having—or even seeking—all the facts. This can manifest as **fortune-telling**, where we make bleak predictions about the future without accounting for all the potential scenarios that could just as easily occur, or **mind-reading**, where we make negative assumptions about how others are thinking or feeling based on our own perceptions.

A familiar example might be how new parents tend to jump to conclusions when their child isn't hitting the same milestones as their peers. This is definitely one of the noisier parts of toddlerhood. If our child's vocabulary isn't at the same level as others at twelve months, we may automatically assume we've done something wrong: we shouldn't have let them watch television so young; we should've bought those flash cards or read them extra bedtime stories. Of course, this line of thinking doesn't account for one glaring fact: all children are different! They grow and learn at their own pace.

The truth is, life is messy and complicated. There are usually myriad reasons why things and people behave the way they do. So instead of attempting to predict the future, we can simply get curious: ask questions and be open to possibilities. We might not get the neat and tidy answer we're looking for, but at least we won't be swimming in the noise of our own assumptions.

> **Journal Prompts:**
>
> • What assumptions do I make about my loved ones' behavior, or the world around me?
>
> • How do I feel when my loved ones jump to conclusions about my behavior? What do I say? What do I want to say?
>
> • What can I tell myself when I start to jump to conclusions, fortune-tell, or mind-read?

MAGNIFICATION AND MINIMIZATION

Magnification, also known as **catastrophizing**, is when we exaggerate how important a certain situation is or how likely a certain outcome is. This is when we dream up a worst-case scenario, amplifying how likely it is to occur and exaggerating what the potential fallout may be. At the same time, we minimize any evidence that contradicts the outcome we're magnifying.

This distortion often comes into play when we're fearful. Say you have a teenage son who was invited to join his friend's family on vacation. You've known this friend for years; you're even friends with his parents. But the vacation in question requires air travel—something you're deathly afraid of. Even though you willingly accept the risk of your son driving himself to school each day—a scenario in which he's statistically far more likely to get hurt—you can't allow him to take this trip, because you know his plane will be the one to disappear over the Atlantic. You're magnifying the most unlikely outcome possible while minimizing the far more likely outcome: that your son will have a lovely vacation, expand his horizons, and return home in one piece.

Journal Prompts:

- *When do I tend to catastrophize?*

- *How do I feel when my loved ones catastrophize? What do I say? What do I want to say?*

- *What can I tell myself when I start to catastrophize?*

EMOTIONAL REASONING

Emotional reasoning occurs when we treat our internal feelings as external facts. Rather than consider the transient nature of emotions or take into account factors beyond our feelings in the immediate moment, we decide that what we feel must be recognized—by us and by others—as objective truth.

This is a common challenge, as our emotions can be quite powerful, convincing, and even overwhelming. And, to be sure, there is some truth to be found in our emotional responses: anger is a common response when we perceive injustice, while sadness can alert us to what we value and care about. However, while emotions can make us aware of our own subjective truths, they are not facts about the nature of reality.

Many of us will feel defensive when we're told that our feelings aren't facts—it's a phrase that's often used to discount the importance of emotions altogether. That's not the intention here, though. What I want you to understand is that when we base our decisions and perspectives on our feelings alone, we're hurting our future selves, who won't always feel the way we do in the moment.

Let's say your child comes home from school distraught over not being invited to a classmate's party. As you wipe away their tears, you notice a pang in your gut. Thoughts start to swirl in your mind, convincing you that this is somehow all your fault. You find yourself sliding down a slippery slope as you begin to find so-called supporting facts for your feelings: *I should have organized more playdates, or connected with the other parents, or thrown more parties.* Unwittingly, you've allowed your feelings to convince you that you're somehow at fault. When you're able to step back and recognize that emotional reasoning is at play, however, you can quickly call to mind the multitude of possible reasons your child wasn't invited to the party—none of which have to do with you.

Our emotions are signals that tell us what needs attending to. There's a reason we may be quick to blame ourselves when our child is disappointed—this in itself is worth further exploration. When we entangle our emotions with our child's experiences, it removes our opportunity to parent in a secure, supportive manner.

The fact is, life will be full of disappointments. It's how we respond to those moments that determines whether we live in noise or effectively block it.

> **Journal Prompts:**
> - *When have my emotions led me to make false conclusions?*
> - *How do I feel when my loved ones engage in emotional reasoning? What do I say? What do I want to say?*
> - *What can I tell myself when I start to use emotional reasoning?*

"SHOULD" STATEMENTS

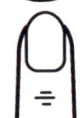

Should. Shouldn't. Must. Ought to. Supposed to. Have to. When one of these words or phrases slips into your thinking, it's time to hit the pause button. While it's common to catch "a case of the shoulds," it's also a clear sign that we're harboring feelings of regret, remorse, envy, and hopelessness.

"Should" statements often occur when we compare ourselves to others, using their experiences as a barometer of our own success. Let's say you have a friend who seems to have done everything "right": she graduated from a top university with high honors, started a successful company, got married, and had two healthy kids—all before the age of thirty. And because this friend of yours managed to reach all these milestones in record time, you now question yourself for not doing the same.

One of the reasons noisy thoughts are so stubborn and repetitive is because they're based partially on facts. Perhaps it's true that your friend went to an esteemed university, founded a Fortune 500 company, and started a family. What's not true is that you have to accomplish the same things, on the same timeline, in order to live a happy life.

We've already established that what works for our friends won't necessarily work for us, and vice versa. We've also learned that what we are—in this case, a successful Ivy League grad with a successful business and a nuclear family—is not *who* we are, and that hitting these life milestones does not guarantee that our friend is happy. It's also not guaranteed that we'll find happiness by following in their footsteps. All of this is as factual as our friend's hard-earned accomplishments. When we start to place expectations on ourselves, we have to be willing to recognize all the facts of a situation—not just the ones that fit our noisy narrative.

It's fruitless to measure ourselves against others, for the simple fact that we're not others—we're ourselves. Each of our lives is a confluence of differing circumstances, upbringings, skills, opportunities, personalities, and countless other variables. It's impossible to live someone else's life, and trying to is a recipe for noise.

We also tend to compare our noise with someone else's happiness, disregarding the difficulties that come along with their unique situation. No one lives a perfect, noise-free existence; we all have our battle wounds to heal, and we never truly know what another person has had to endure to become who they are. When we find ourselves wishing for someone else's blessings and challenges, it may be time to remember all that we have to be grateful for in our own lives.

However, comparison is just one way to catch a case of the shoulds. Another is when we ruminate over and regret our past decisions. "I should've known they weren't the right match for me. If I'd married someone else, I would be happy now." That's what we tell ourselves, even though there's no guarantee that marrying a different person would have resulted in a lasting and happy relationship.

Hindsight is 20/20. The shoulds represent our desire for a time machine—a chance to go back and set things right. It works in the movies, right? Well, no. The ultimate lesson of time-travel movies is that we're not supposed to mess with the past—and things go sideways when we try.

There's no way for any of us to know what we don't know. We learn through experience. It's easy to say we should've known better, but the only way to learn what "better" means is to have the experience in the first place. Once we have that experience, we can make different decisions in the future—but we need experiences that help us learn and grow first. When I find myself having a case of the shoulds, I remember that there are no mistakes, just experiences.

Journal Prompts:

- *What regrets have I found it difficult to move on from?*
- *How do I feel when my loved ones speak in "should" statements? What do I say? What do I want to say?*
- *What can I tell myself when I start to use "should" statements?*

LABELING

This is overgeneralizing taken to the extreme. It's when we label ourselves or others based on one negative experience or misstep. We didn't just lose our child for five seconds at the grocery store; we're a "bad parent." We didn't just stay up too late the night before a big presentation; we're an "irresponsible idiot."

Imagine your child made a Herculean effort on a school project. They worked diligently for weeks, quizzing you over dinner with facts they learned and improving their writing and research skills. But when they finally hand in the project, the outcome isn't what they'd hoped for. Their teacher gives them an average grade, and they give themselves a new label: "I'm bad at school." Or, worse: "I'm dumb."

Of course, this label discounts the efforts they made, the skills they sharpened, and the things they learned along the way. That the ultimate result didn't meet someone else's criteria is only part of the story. Their dedication and willingness to try hard are worth celebrating, regardless of the final result.

Do you remember your sixth-grade test scores? You most likely don't. However, you remember the importance of learning how to study, how to complete a task, and how to deal with its consequences. Labeling is what happens when we focus a great deal on the outcome while discounting the process that makes it all possible. Success isn't determined by outcome. Success is determined by how we show up—in this case, with passion, dedication, and a willingness to learn. Success is about the process, what we learn and pick up along the way.

> **Journal Prompts:**
>
> • What labels have I given myself in the past? What do I consider myself to be "bad" at?
>
> • How do I feel when my loved ones label themselves? What do I say? What do I want to say?
>
> • What can I tell myself when I start to label?

FALLACY OF CHANGE

These distortions come in two forms. The first is when we believe we have the ability and responsibility to change someone else's moods, feelings, or behaviors. Often, this stems from a good place: we all want to see our loved ones happy and thriving, and when they're not, we feel compelled to intervene. It's normal to not want to see our loved ones suffering, but when we go so far as to believe that we're uniquely qualified to rescue them from themselves, we've gone too far.

We can see how harmful this mindset becomes in the context of addiction. A person who's married to someone struggling with alcoholism may believe it's their job to make their partner stop drinking: they'll hide the credit cards, pour the liquor down the toilet, refuse intimacy, or even threaten to leave. Then, when their spouse continues to drink anyway, they wonder what they are doing wrong.

They don't realize that even their best efforts to control their spouse will be fruitless because, ultimately, it's not within their power to control their partner. Only the addicted person can do that. All they can do is take control of themselves, even if that means detaching from the situation and allowing their spouse to experience the unmediated consequences of their drinking.

The second fallacy of change is our feeling that we *can't* change—that our life is beyond our control. It's always someone else's fault, or maybe our childhood is to blame, or it's fate—one way or another, we're not in the driver's seat of our own life, and there's no way we can improve the situation. When these thoughts take control, they make a person feel stuck, hopeless, and frozen.

This dynamic plays out on the other side of addiction. People who struggle with substance abuse are often plagued with noisy thoughts; the belief that they're already too far gone to change is especially common. Many of these people feel painted into a corner by their past; they can't imagine a future that involves forgiveness. They believe there's nothing they can do to change who they've been—and even if there was, they believe they don't deserve it.

Once again, the focus needs to be on the process, not the outcome. As long as you refuse to take one step forward, you're not just afraid that you can't change—you're all but guaranteeing it. Instead, give yourself grace and just take one step at a time. No one is capable of transforming overnight—and even if we were, we'd miss out on all the wonderful things we should be learning from the process.

Journal Prompts:

- *Whose moods, behaviors, and actions do I find myself wishing I could change?*

- *How do I feel when my loved ones engage in the fallacy of change? What do I say? What do I want to say?*

- *What can I tell myself when I start to try to change others? What can I tell myself when I don't feel in control of my own life?*

PERSONALIZATION

This is the compulsion to make yourself responsible for things that have nothing to do with you. You take the blame, or even beat yourself up, for events that are rationally out of your control and impossible for you to influence.

Your daughter gets into a fight with her best friend, and you respond with so much guilt, it's as though you personally instigated it. Your wife comes home from work in a bad mood, and you instantly believe it must be something you did; you start "making it up" to her and then feel hurt when she just wants to be left alone. You take the blame for traffic jams you didn't cause, for baseball games getting rained out, and for offenses you didn't commit.

Personalization causes us to center ourselves in situations that have nothing to do with us. Not only do we unnecessarily burden ourselves when we do this, but we also fail to recognize that people exist outside of their relation to us. Not everything is about us—and that's a good thing!

Journal Prompts:

- *Do I tend to take responsibility for things that have nothing to do with me?*

- *How do I feel when my loved ones engage in personalization? What do I say? What do I want to say?*

- *What can I tell myself when I start engaging in personalization?*

CHILD OR ADULT, IT'S NATURAL TO FEEL AFRAID SOMETIMES.

CHAPTER 9
BECOMING FEARLESS

Youth is marked by a certain fearlessness. Whether they're dominating the monkey bars on the playground, learning to cartwheel, or making unexpected yet inspired fashion statements, kids have mastered the art of what I call "fearless freedom." They are bold, curious, and, above all, resilient.

The weight of adult responsibilities makes it easy to forget that, as kids, we used to be fearless. It's not that we were never scared of anything—in fact, more like the opposite. When you're a kid, many things seem scary, from an oddly shaped shadow to the furnace in the basement. But we kids didn't fear *fear*. We talked about what scared us, we asked an adult for help, and eventually we moved on.

Child or adult, it's natural to feel afraid sometimes. Fear is a human instinct, not something we mature out of. What we do tend to outgrow is our openness to fear: we don't want to identify it, label it, or talk about it. Oftentimes we don't even consider asking for help. We fear the feeling of fear itself.

WHAT IS FEAR?

Fear is an innate response to danger—real or imagined—and it manifests physically, mentally, emotionally, and spiritually. We feel fear in our hearts, minds, bodies, and spirits.

No human being can escape the experience of fear. In fact, we're evolutionarily hardwired for it. For our caveman ancestors, the ability to recognize threats meant the difference between life and death. Knowing when to fight, flee, or freeze was a matter of survival. Even though modern life is far safer than it was for earlier humans, our primordial instinct to anticipate and respond to danger—our instinct for self-preservation—remains intact. We can't escape it.

Many of the fears we can easily identify in our own lives take on some sort of physical form. It starts when we're kids: our fear of the unknown manifests as our fear of the dark, creepy basement; our fear of losing control manifests as a fear of heights. When fear is triggered or represented by a physical object or experience, it's easier to identify and address. If you're afraid of heights, for example, you visit your cousin's new apartment with the stunning rooftop views but avoid the balcony, seek therapy to explore the source of the aversion, or join an online community for people working through similar fears.

But what about those fears of a more abstract nature—the ones you can't identify, let alone avoid? What about the fears that follow you everywhere you go, clinging to you like secondhand smoke?

Abstract fears are much more difficult to identify, because they're subjective. They stem from our personal thoughts, particularly the noisy ones. They also disguise themselves in other emotions, like anger or disgust. Sometimes we can pinpoint a moment that made us fearful and left us that way; sometimes it takes a lot more effort and soul-searching to find the source. Those hard-to-identify fears are so challenging because without understanding the problem, we can't find the solution.

These sneaky fears are often far more debilitating than those with a concrete, physical form. They're part of our daily existence. After all, how often are you surrounded by snakes or forced to stand on an unsecured rooftop? Hopefully not often! But how often are you surrounded by noisy thoughts? Every second of every day.

You're afraid of letting down the ones you love. You're afraid of not living up to the expectations of your spouse, friends, kids, or culture. You're afraid of failure. You're afraid of success. You can't pinpoint a specific object or moment that causes the fear to rise up inside of you, but the feeling is as real and frightening as looking out over a balcony on the fifteenth floor. It's immersive. It chases you, seeping into every aspect of your thought process and life.

Remember: fear is what helped our caveman ancestors survive. Their fear of predators, floods, droughts, and other disasters developed because encountering these environmental threats put them at real physical risk. Fear is our brain's way of protecting us from these perceived threats. The big difference between us and the cavemen is that we no longer encounter life-threatening scenarios on a daily basis. Feeling fear no longer means our lives are in imminent danger—even though it still feels that way.

> **COMMON FEAR RESPONSES**
> - **FIGHT**: *"It's time to attack!"*
> - **FLIGHT**: *"I'm outta here!"*
> - **FREEZE**: *"I feel trapped in my body!"*

WRESTLING WITH IRRATIONAL FEAR

Modern fear is like walking into a room and being struck by an awful smell. You can't see what's causing it, yet you know it's real, because your senses are on high alert. All you can think about is how to get rid of it—if only you could figure out what "it" is.

As you search the room for old food, dirty clothes, or a rodent that met its demise behind the couch, the smell continues to assault you. Whatever you were planning to do before has been forgotten; your only options now are to fight (keep searching for the source of the stank), flee (find another room to hang out in, for however long it takes a dead rat to decompose), or freeze (maybe, if you stay very still, the smell will lose interest and find someone else to harass).

Fear is similar. It can wreak havoc on our lives, even while we have no clue where it's coming from or how to make it go away.

In some sense, our prehistoric ancestors had it easy when it came to fear. It makes sense for your heart to start racing when an enormous, carnivorous creature is charging toward you. Fear in the twenty-first century is different: today, most of our fears are irrational and outsized reactions to the non-life-threatening experiences in our lives. Like our hunt for the phantom smell, finding the source of our fears is not a quick and easy task.

There's an old poem called "Antigonish," by Hughes Mearns. The opening lines are rather apropos:

> *Yesterday, upon the stair,*
> *I met a man who wasn't there*
> *He wasn't there again today*
> *I wish, I wish he'd go away*

Our fears don't have to be rational for them to cause us anguish, and we can't ignore them in hopes that they'll just disappear. They may not alert us to any real threats we're facing, but our most debilitating fears are a prime indicator of the noisy thoughts holding us back from the life we want to live.

This can be hard to recognize, because we often justify our fears with facts. It's a fact that falling from a tall building will likely kill you—but that doesn't mean standing on a safe, enclosed balcony is dangerous. Linking facts to your fears may justify them in the moment, but misusing facts to explain them away only obscures the true reason you're afraid.

WHAT ARE YOU AFRAID OF?

We're all afraid of different things. Think about your greatest, most persistent fear. Even if you dig deep inside yourself, you may still struggle to describe it or share it with others. You know you're afraid, but you can't pinpoint why or how it started. Even the thought of letting someone else in on it is nerve-racking.

Now think of how your four-year-old self would respond to the question "What are you afraid of?" You can even ask your own kids what they would say. Kids don't miss a beat when it comes to this stuff. They immediately say, "I'm afraid of the dark!" or "I'm afraid of monsters!" or "I'm afraid of thunder!"

Kids can more clearly express their fears—and, as a result, they can more easily move beyond them. It's easy to attribute that to a child's innocence, but it's deeper than that.

Part of growing up in a healthy environment is having adults around who can comfort us when we're afraid. As kids, we recognize that adults are in control and can take care of everything; they possess the power to erase any and every fear. As a mom, I can open the closet door and banish any malevolent spirits hiding within. My words alone can chase away the scariest of monsters. If one of my kids is afraid of the dark, I can put their mind at ease with the flick of a night-light. My kids know I'm there for them, unconditionally and always.

When our kids are afraid, it's easy to be objective and cool-headed because we know their fearful perceptions are not reality. We have a much harder time being objective when it comes to our own adult fears. To us, they're as real as the boogeyman that once hid under our bed. Our fears can make us feel like we're incapable of doing for ourselves what we're able to do for our kids—but the truth is, each and every one of us has the ability to quiet the thoughts that make us run, hide, or even attack out of fear. We can learn to be fearless, to turn on the night-light within and see that there's nothing to be afraid of.

The power to live fearlessly resides within us, and always has. When we choose to live a life without fear, we're empowered to pursue our dreams to the fullest. And who wouldn't want that?

OUR FEAR OF SUCCESS

When my eight-year-old son was asked by his teacher what he'd like to be when he grows up, he responded without missing a beat: he'll be a baker with his own bakery, a professor, a scientist, and an artist. When she asked how he plans to do all that, he said, "All at once, of course," without an ounce of trepidation.

I'm sure many of us can remember saying something similar at that age. I know I did. As kids, we grow up believing we can be an astronaut, a champion athlete, or the doctor who cures cancer. There's no fear, no question in our minds: we've got what it takes—and we'll do what it takes—to achieve our dreams. But then what so many people call "reality" sets in. Whether it's at home, at school, at work, or among friends, we start to hear things like:

- *"You can't be a pro athlete. The chances of being drafted are slim to none."*
- *"You can't go to outer space. You wear glasses."*
- *"You can't become a doctor. It's too much school for you."*

Slowly we start to doubt ourselves and our capabilities. The dreams that once motivated us begin to look foolish, childish, and impractical. As a result, we start looking for an alternative path—an easier, safer path. It's not what we would've chosen for ourselves, and it doesn't light our heart on fire, but at least we won't look silly when we fail. Long story short, we've given in to fear.

SIGNS OF FEARFUL BEHAVIOR

- Many of us fear success because we've been taught that "what goes up must come down." We've bought into the idea that the higher we fly, the harder we'll fall—and we'll only have ourselves to blame when we inevitably do.

- We may shy away from success because we were taught from a young age to be content with mediocrity—and that wishing for anything more is selfish, immoral, or just plain delusional.

- We may feel ashamed of having big dreams, afraid of being seen as egotistical and full of ourselves. How many of us were told not to get too big for our britches as children?

- We may have grown up with parents who had to defer their own dreams and expect us to do the same, or without role models to show us that what we want to achieve is possible.

Basically, our fear of success tells us that aiming too high is a guaranteed recipe for disappointment—if not today, then at some later date. But in truth, none of us can predict the future. (Remember: the idea that we're clairvoyant is a cognitive distortion, a noisy thought.) The reality is that nothing about tomorrow, next week, or five years from now is set in stone. We don't have to live as though our upbringing, our education, or any other circumstances beyond our control have anything to do with where we're headed or what we may be able to accomplish.

So many of us are so afraid of "heights" that we'd rather settle than even try to reach our goals. We're okay with not taking risks, because we don't want to face the imagined consequences of doing so. But in order to live fearlessly, we have to overcome this mentality. There's too much at stake. This is about more than missing an opportunity here and there—it's about missing the chance to reach our fullest, highest potential.

MAKING OUR DREAMS COME TRUE

The truth is, you can achieve any dream you're willing to pursue—if you put in the work. The most important thing is to pursue something that fulfills you. Don't worry about how you'll eventually monetize it, or how practical it is. If you pursue something that drains you, no dollar amount will ever be enough to satisfy you. But if you pursue something that feeds your soul, you'll find that its presence in your life is priceless—even if you never make a penny doing it.

So often, we abandon our dreams in favor of "practicality." We're afraid that pursuing our dreams means we'll go broke, that our parents won't approve of our choices, or that our professional peers or friends will judge us for coloring outside the lines. How can we live fearlessly when our car payment, phone bill, rent, and insurance are all due within seven days of one another? These are rational concerns, but it's irrational to be afraid of the bottom constantly dropping out. It's also irrational to design our lives to meet other people's standards—not to mention impossible.

There are so many fears that prevent us from becoming whole, and it would be easy to make excuses as to why we need to give in to them. We think there's something noble about sacrificing what brings us joy. But when we defer our dreams for too long, it doesn't just affect us—it affects everyone we encounter. We start to resent ourselves and everyone around us—even our loved ones. Maybe even especially our loved ones! What's noble about that?

Throughout our lives, we receive all kinds of messages—some subtle, some explicit—that pursuing our dreams is selfish, but nothing could be further from the truth. Striving toward a meaningful goal gives us the enthusiasm and energy we need to enjoy life rather than endure it. It also gives us the wisdom and inner security to support others as they pursue their dreams—and in a culture where so many people settle for less than what they want and deserve, that encouragement means the world. When we pursue what most inspires us, we paint our lives—and the lives of others—with possibility.

So, no, making your dreams come true is not inherently selfish. But there are selfish ways to go about it. Pursuing your dreams doesn't mean throwing all caution to the wind and not caring whether your mortgage is paid and your kids are fed. You don't need to toss your whole life in the garbage disposal to work toward your dreams. In fact, our loved ones can be our most valuable supporters as we chase our highest potential—they're not problems to work around as we embark on our quest for success. There are options in between living your dream and living a nightmare; it just requires a little creative thinking to see them.

One of my dreams has been to write this book. As I'd go about my day, running errands and driving children here and there, I'd find myself chatting with my family about the latest chapter or idea—even as I convinced myself that they'd vote me off the island if I mentioned it again! Thankfully, they often responded with interest and encouragement. I say "often" because occasionally the response was an eye roll—I have teenagers—or surprise (*She's still doing that?!*). I point this out because living fearlessly doesn't mean living a life of rainbows and unicorns. On the contrary, pursuing your dream is often messy. It requires us to live in the gray.

Many of us feel that we simply don't have time to pursue anything that rejuvenates us, and that leads us to write off our dreams entirely. That's all-or-nothing thinking, though. Instead of disowning your dreams, why not take baby steps toward them? Devote forty-five minutes a day (or night) to working at it. Explore, research, save, and plan for the future. Talk to your partner (or a parent or a friend) and see if they can help find ways to free up your time or otherwise support you. Learn about the people who've achieved what you're hoping to accomplish—or even better, talk to them. You'll soon realize that they're human, just like you.

Maybe that's the most important thing to remember: that the people who are living your dream are people like you, no more and no less. When we dive below the surface and past the superficialities, we discover there's no real difference between any of us. We all breathe the same air and have the same basic needs. I have a friend whose beloved grandfather gave him some invaluable advice: "Think about whoever you admire. They have to get up in the morning and put their pants on one leg at a time, just like you do. The only difference is they didn't give up on the dream. They put in the work."

That work is the process. It's life. It's fun. It's everything.

LIVING FEARLESSLY

Spend ten minutes in any schoolyard or playground and you'll witness shining examples of what life can feel like when you triumph over your fears. The unmitigated joy of a child who's just accomplished some daring feat is exhilarating and contagious. We're all born with that kind of fearless freedom, and we don't have to lose it just because we grew up.

In this next exercise, we're going to identify your fears, challenge them, and help you adopt the fearless-freedom mindset you need to make your wildest dreams come true. All you need are a pen, paper, and some time to reflect. Let's go!

EXERCISE: LIVING FEARLESSLY

1 STEP 1: IDENTIFY YOUR FEARS

Start by identifying and writing down your greatest, most persistent fears, both concrete and abstract. Some fears will come to mind right away, while others will require you to probe a little deeper. Our stubborn human pride makes it hard to admit what we're truly afraid of. So often, we're told that admitting to fear is admitting to weakness, when really it's the exact opposite. Facing our fears—flicking on our inner night-light—is the only way to see them in the cold light of day and diminish the power they have over us.

Start by reflecting on this common list of fears, marking any that resonate with you. Make note of any specific people, places, experiences, and events that trigger your fears.

Common Concrete Fears

- *Fear of flying*
- *Fear of heights*
- *Fear of bridges*
- *Fear of drowning*
- *Fear of fire*
- *Fear of spiders*
- *Fear of snakes*
- *Fear of small, enclosed spaces*
- *Fear of social events*
- *Fear of public speaking*
- *Fear of blood*
- *Fear of doctors*
- *Fear of dogs*
- *Fear of clowns*

Common Abstract Fears

- *Fear of failure*
- *Fear of success*
- *Fear of rejection*
- *Fear of intimacy*
- *Fear of not belonging*
- *Fear of the unknown*
- *Fear of mediocrity*
- *Fear of change*
- *Fear of losing control*

Reflect on the following prompts to continue building your list:

- *What situations, people, or events do you find yourself avoiding or resisting? Public speaking? Airplanes? Going to the dentist? Conflict with your loved ones? Write down any scenarios you tend to resist and consider what feelings you're attempting to avoid when you do so.*
- *How do you know when you're afraid? How does your body respond? What thoughts run through your mind?*
- *Do you have any recurring nightmares or stress dreams? What happens in them? Is there a theme? What do you think the core message is?*
- *What are some things you would like to experience but haven't? What is stopping you from trying? What do you think would happen if you tried?*

2 STEP 2: ASSESSING YOUR FEARS

Now we're going to dive deeper and attempt to locate the source of your fears. Working your way down the list, answer the following questions:

- *When was the first time you remember feeling this fear? What people, events, and memories are attached to it?*
- *How does this fear manifest in your life today? What situations, people, or places trigger this fear?*
- *What noisy thoughts do you have that relate to this fear? Does your fear of failure tell you not to bother taking risks, because you already know how things will turn out (fortune-telling)? Does your fear of rejection tell you all your relationships will fail, simply because the last one didn't work out (overgeneralization)? Consult the "cognitive distortions" descriptions from the previous chapter for a quick refresher. You may find you have more than one noisy thought triggered by a single fear—write down any that are relevant.*

3 STEP 3: ANALYZING YOUR FEARS

You're now going to interrogate and challenge each fear on your list, and the noisy thoughts that accompany it. Pretend you're a lawyer, hired to mount the strongest case possible against each of your fears. Use the following reflection questions to help build your argument.

- *What's the worst-case scenario you associate with this fear? What's the statistical likelihood of it coming true? If you had to bet $5,000 on how likely it is to happen, would you bet on it or against it?*
- *Is this fear rational? What are some objective facts that challenge your narrative?*
- *What would you think if someone you love came to you and expressed this fear? Would you think they were justified? What would you tell them to put them at ease?*
- *When you've had to confront this fear in the past, what was the outcome?*

4 STEP 4: EVALUATE YOUR COPING MECHANISMS

There are many ways to respond to fear, but most of them are not effective or rational. List the ways you currently address your fears when they rise to the surface. Here are a few prompts to get you started:

- *Do you avoid thinking about it or engaging with it?*
- *Do you seek advice?*
- *Do you distract yourself with work or other responsibilities?*
- *Do you run away?*
- *Do you fixate, overthink, obsess, and ruminate yourself into a panic attack?*
- *Do you pretend nothing is wrong?*
- *Do you research your fear?*
- *Do you isolate yourself?*
- *Do you let shame or embarrassment take over?*

Now that you have a list of your most common responses, rank their efficiency from 1 to 10 (with 1 being "counterproductive" and 10 being "very effective"). Which, if any, would you recommend to a loved one?

Remember: fear enables us to avoid dangerous situations. Therefore, some coping mechanisms are appropriate in specific situations but not in others. If a car is speeding toward us, for example, we want our heart to pound, our breath to quicken, and our legs to carry us to a safe location. What we don't want is to have that same reaction to an unnerving tweet or a headline in a newspaper.

Fear is useful when it prevents us from getting hit by a car, but it harms us emotionally, socially, and physically when the stakes are nowhere near as high. This is what happens when we allow our fears to run wild. The good news is that we can just as easily pick up the reins and steer ourselves back on course.

5 STEP 5: MAKE A PLAN

While we can't predict or control the future, we can develop skills and strategies that help us feel capable and confident in our ability to overcome whatever challenges life throws our way.

What we want to do here is pair a specific tactic with each of the fears you listed earlier. The below list is meant to provide inspiration only—feel free to get creative if they don't address your specific fears.

Instead of letting my fears run wild, I can . . .

- *Research my fears and triggers. By understanding and demystifying my fear, I can come up with strategies to deal with it in a concrete way.*
- *Bring myself back to the present. Fear is often not about what's happening in the present, but imagining what could happen in the future. When I bring my focus to my body and the room I'm in, it can remind me that my fear is most real in my head. Focus on the here and now, not the if and then.*
- *Talk to experts who understand the issue better than I do. I can see a doctor about the health anxieties I experience, or talk to a therapist about ways to build my resilience.*

- *Journal my thoughts and reassess them later. This will give me the distance I need from my fears to see them rationally and objectively.*
- *Investigate reality. Rather than look for facts that justify my fears, I can look for facts that refute them.*
- *Dissect my fears. By breaking my fear down into smaller components, I can make it more manageable and easier to understand.*
- *Turn to my A-Team. I can lean on a therapist, spouse, friend, family member, or spiritual adviser I trust to help me work through my feelings.*
- *Talk about it. Sharing my feelings and thoughts with others takes away their power. If I don't have anyone on my A-Team to turn to about this topic, I can seek out online forums or support groups for people who understand what I'm going through.*
- *Coach myself through it. I can comfort myself, congratulate myself for sitting with a difficult feeling, and give myself recognition for surviving it.*

6 STEP 6: ENJOY!

Now that you've gained a thorough understanding of the role fear plays in your life and revamped your approach to it, you're fully equipped to turn on the night-light the next time it comes to visit.

As Franklin D. Roosevelt famously said, "The only thing we have to fear is fear itself." Fear isn't our enemy; it plays an important role in our lives and doesn't have to stop us from living our best ones.

STEP 1	**STEP 2**	**STEP 3**
Identify your fears	*Assesss your fears*	*Analyze your fears*

STEP 4	**STEP 5**	**STEP 6**
Your coping mechanisms	*Make a plan*	*ENJOY!* *Enjoying fearless freedom takes practice. Be patient with yourself as you learn to remove obstacles.*

YOU HAVE EVERYTHING YOU NEED TO BE HAPPY.

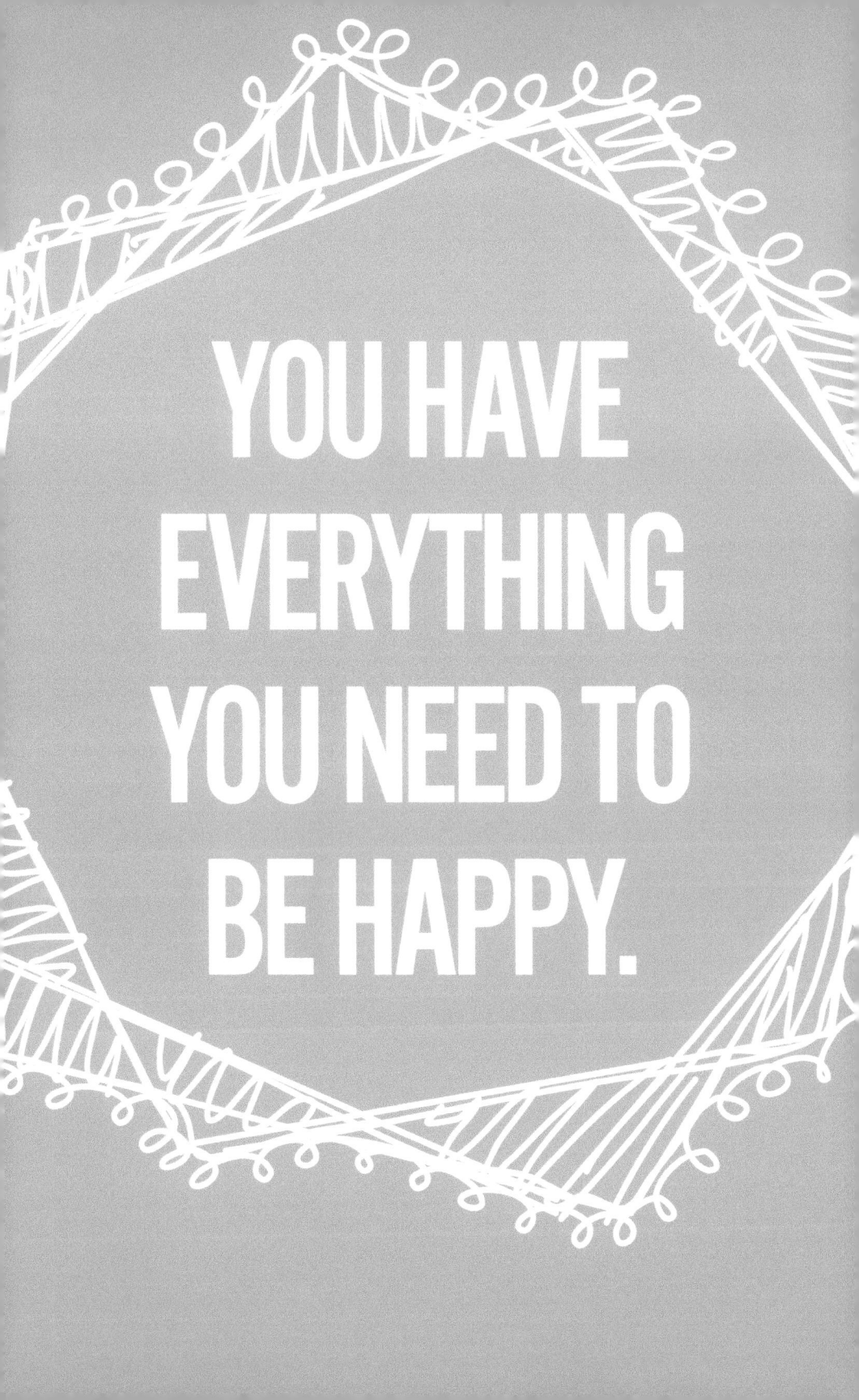

CHAPTER 10
BLOCKING THE NOISE FOR GOOD

To begin our final chapter together, I first want to express my gratitude. It was my great honor to present these perspectives to you in the hope that they may help you block the noise and live your best life. Thank you for trusting me and for joining me on this journey. To say that I'm appreciative of your time and trust is an understatement. I hope that after all our time together, you consider me—and this book—a part of your village and your A-Team!

Now, let's take a look at how far you've come.

First, you met noise. Chances are you were already well acquainted, but meeting noise gave you a name for your experiences. Now you can identify it—and its sources—in your own life. You became aware of what's been preventing you from achieving a baseline of happiness.

Next, we explored your relationships. We identified the roles you play in the lives of others and the joy and the noise you experience in those roles. We learned how to detach and cope with difficult people in our lives, and how to accept people and situations for who and what they are.

You came into contact with your Gracious Self and identified the multifaceted members of your A-Team—the friends, family, and professionals who support, augment, and enhance your happiness.

You also got to know yourself, hopefully like never before. Through deep personal analysis, you began to truly grasp what makes you happy and what makes you tick. You learned how cognitive distortions exert a profound impact on how you approach life. Finally, you confronted your lifelong fears, recovered your deep-seated dreams, and learned to embrace the fearless freedom that's always been your birthright.

In short, you learned to block the noise. And I could not be happier for you.

Just as you discovered your personal happiness through the pages in this book, I discovered my own happiness through the same process. My goal in developing this program was to empower anyone, anywhere, to go on their own journey of self-discovery. Implementing the tenets of this program in my own life reframed the way I viewed my existence and the world around me. It enabled me to be unapologetically myself.

It all comes down to emphasizing the aspects of yourself that serve your happiness and allowing the rest to fall away. It really is that simple. The hard part is letting go and allowing it to be simple.

If there's anything you take away from this book, I hope it's the knowledge that you already have at your disposal the tools you need to live your best life. You don't need to "fix" yourself or anyone else—nothing is wrong with you! Nor do you need to search for happiness or answers. I've witnessed too many of my loved ones dissect themselves in order to "figure it out," not realizing how debilitating and discouraging a process like that can be. There's nothing to search for or figure out. You already have everything you need at your fingertips.

JUST BE.

DON'T OVERTHINK EVERY MISTAKE OR BAD DAY.

JUST BE.

DON'T RELIVE THE PAST OR WISH FOR A TIME MACHINE.

JUST BE.

DON'T FOCUS ON EVERY TINY FLAW YOU PERCEIVE IN YOURSELF AND OTHERS.

JUST BE.

BLOCKING THE NOISE: THE DAILY PRACTICE

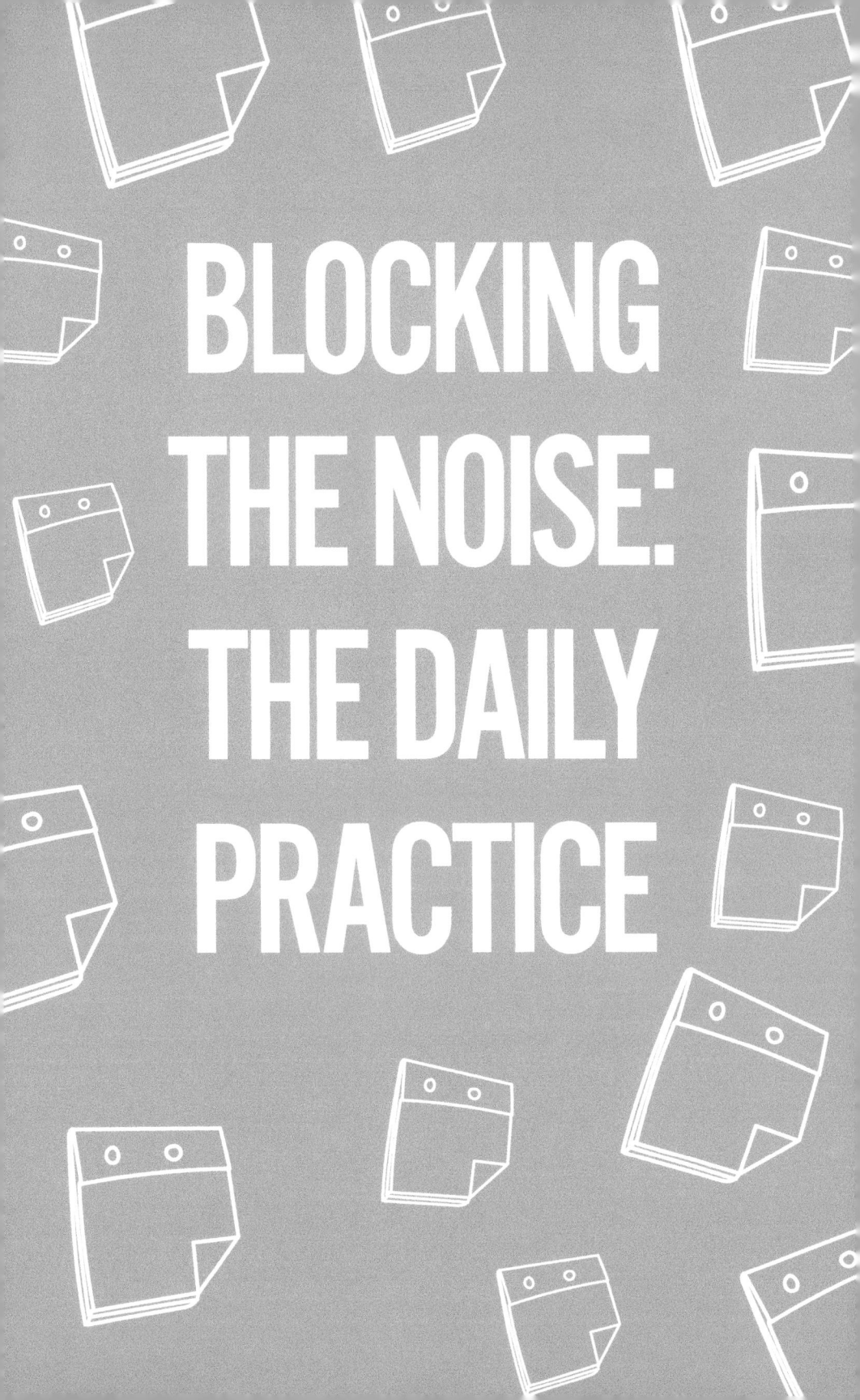

I was delighted when my youngest came up with a points system for our household chores: it incentivized him and his siblings to help out around the house, sure—but also, I was *crushing it*. That is, until I showed him the hundreds of points I'd racked up, only for him to point out that I had zero points in one particular category: self-care.

If you're like me, the concept of self-care wasn't spoken about in your childhood home; it certainly didn't coexist with the rest of your chores. But my son was right to include it in our points system: even if self-care is not a chore in the traditional sense, many of us will do anything to avoid it, treating it with the same disdain we have for cleaning the litter box or taking out the garbage.

The big difference is that we'll still do our daily chores, however begrudgingly, while making self-care take a back seat to the myriad tasks on our to-do list. The truth is, daily self-care is required for our happiness, the same way flossing our teeth is required for our dental hygiene. You might not always feel like doing it, but with enough practice, it will become a habit—one you'll later thank yourself for developing.

So to help you incorporate self-care into your routine, I want to leave you with a daily practice that will help you care for yourself and center your happiness, each and every day. The Blocking the Noise Daily Practice consists of two parts: a morning routine and an evening routine. It's designed to bring focus and balance to your physical, spiritual, and socio-emotional well-being—the core components of your happiness.

SETTING YOURSELF UP FOR SUCCESS

Starting a new routine can be challenging, especially when you don't have a plan. So, before you dive into your new morning routine, let's review what you'll need to be successful.

For your morning routine, you will need . . .

- **At least half an hour.** As a mom to three kids (and a wife and a professional and a friend . . . the list goes on), I know what it's like to struggle to find even thirty seconds for yourself, let alone thirty minutes. But it's not impossible. You may need to wake up earlier than usual, or avoid answering your emails the moment you open your eyes, but you can do it. And while it may take some time to adjust, I know you'll grow to treasure this sacred time to yourself. (And if you've tried to carve out thirty minutes and it's just not taking, start smaller and work your way up—any dedicated time for yourself is better than none at all!)

- **An uncluttered, distraction-free space.** This can be anywhere in your home. All that matters is that, for thirty minutes, you're in a place where your kids, pets, and partner can't reach you. I say "reach you" with a grain of salt. As a mom, I am tethered to my phone. Ideally we could lock our phone away for thirty minutes and forget all about it. However, if just the idea of being without your phone fills you with noise, bring it along. Try setting it to "do not disturb" or airplane mode. Remember, it is what works for you and you alone. Choose a space that stimulates your happiness and is free of anything that will impact your ability to focus on yourself.

- **Comfortable clothes.** Wear something cozy and unrestrictive: pajamas and a robe, a favorite pair of leggings, or a classic sweatsuit are all great options.

- **To set the mood.** Is the room the right temperature? Do you want the window blinds open or closed? Do you have a favorite candle or incense you want to light? A favorite tea to drink in the morning? Stock up on whatever you need to create a relaxing space for yourself.

- **A pen and journal or notebook,** to record your daily reflections in.

You may also choose to invest in additional tools to augment your experience. Some of my favorites are:

- A yoga mat
- A foam roller for stretching
- Noise-canceling headphones or earplugs
- An eye mask
- A cozy blanket
- A kitchen timer (if you decide not to use your phone)

PART 1: THE MORNING ROUTINE

1 Get yourself situated. Adjust the thermostat, light the candle, brew the tea.

2 Engage in a brief stretching exercise or yoga routine.

3 Dim the lights and settle into a comfortable sitting position.

4 Breathe in and out, deeply and slowly, for ten minutes. Try to hold each inhale and exhale for five seconds as you find the right pattern for you and your body. If you notice any pain or discomfort in your body during this step, try to direct your breath toward it, sending healing energy toward the pain. Keep your muscles relaxed and monitor that your breath is gently flowing from your diaphragm. It is extraordinary how the simple monitoring of our breath quickly calms the mind.

> **Quick tip:** *If you're new to meditation or breathing exercises, you may need to work your way up to ten minutes. Try the breathing exercise for two minutes, adding two-minute increments each week until you reach ten minutes. Feel free to go longer from there!*

> **Quick tip:** *As you focus on your breath, you may notice thoughts passing through your mind. Don't worry about this. Thoughts should come into your mind. You were made to think! The trick is to not hold too tightly to any of the thoughts you notice during this exercise. Allow them to come in and out of your mind with the same rhythm as your breath. In and out. In and out.*

5 Raise the lights and grab your pen and journal. It's time to focus on your thoughts, which will come in many forms: words, images, people, events, and feelings, to name a few. Set your timer for five minutes and write down everything that comes into your mind. Try not to overthink, analyze, or edit what you're writing down—right now you're simply taking notes.

6 When your five-minute timer goes off, turn to a fresh page and divide it into two columns: **happy** and **noisy**. Select three noisy thoughts and three happy thoughts that emerged while you were journaling, and list them in the appropriate columns.

> **Quick tip:** *Noise is defined as any person, place, feeling, thought, word, event, or object that gives you a feeling of discomfort or unease. The noisy thoughts you select for the next exercise are things that don't make you happy. Meanwhile, the happy thoughts you select should be those that spontaneously brought a smile to your face or a feeling of warmth in your soul as you reviewed your journal entry.*

> **Quick tip:** *Be careful not to judge your noisy items. People often struggle with this step because they feel certain things should make them happy that, in fact, don't. This is a space for you to be honest with yourself, so don't hold anything back.*

7 Reflect on the items in your noisy column. Refer to your "cognitive distortions" descriptions to identify any unhelpful noisy patterns you find in your thinking and use the techniques you've learned in this book to reframe your noisy thoughts.

> **Quick tip:** *Be gentle with yourself as you become aware of the areas of your life and self that are in need of change. As always, avoid engaging in self-blame, self-hate, or self-criticism. Remember: this is a journey of enlightenment. Every aspect of yourself is a critical part of creating your true, happy self.*

8 Take a mental snapshot—or a literal snapshot, with your phone—of the three things you listed in your happy column. Consciously think about the items on your list as you go through your day, and return to it when you start having noisy thoughts. Make your happiness a priority.

9 Use your list to identify trends and create a concrete plan that nurtures your personal happiness, each and every day.

> **Quick tip:** *Remember, happiness requires focus on your physical, spiritual, and socio-emotional well-being—all three need attention and maintenance. Therefore, your happiness plan might include eating a healthy, delicious lunch or taking a walk around the park after dinner (physical well-being); reading a spiritual book or setting aside time to focus on your breath (spiritual well-being); and having a long phone call with someone from your A-Team (socio-emotional well-being).*

Eventually, the items on your happiness list will move from conscious to subconscious thought. You will no longer have to go through your day focusing on what makes you happy, because your subconscious will guide you to them.

HAPPY COLUMN	NOISY COLUMN

PART 2:
THE EVENING ROUTINE

You've already done the heavy lifting with your morning routine—now all you need is ten minutes at the end of each day to reflect.

1 Grab your journal and settle back into the quiet, happy space where you started your day.

2 Reflect on your noisy list. How did it influence your day? Did it influence your day? You may find that the thoughts you were struggling with in the morning never came to pass—you may have forgotten about them entirely!

3 Reflect on your happy list. Did it help you throughout the day? Do you have anything to change or add?

4 Reflect on your happiness. What did you do for your physical well-being? What about your spiritual and socio-emotional well-being?

5 To close out the day, list three things you love about yourself. Remind yourself how incredible and perfect you are, just as you are.

THREE THINGS YOU LOVE ABOUT YOURSELF

As always, love yourself, be kind to yourself, and remember that life is for enjoying, not enduring.

With love, gratitude, and respect,

Dr. Angelina

HAPPY REFLECTION

NOISY REFLECTION

"LIFE IS FOR ENJOYING AND NOT ENDURING."

—DR. ANGELINA

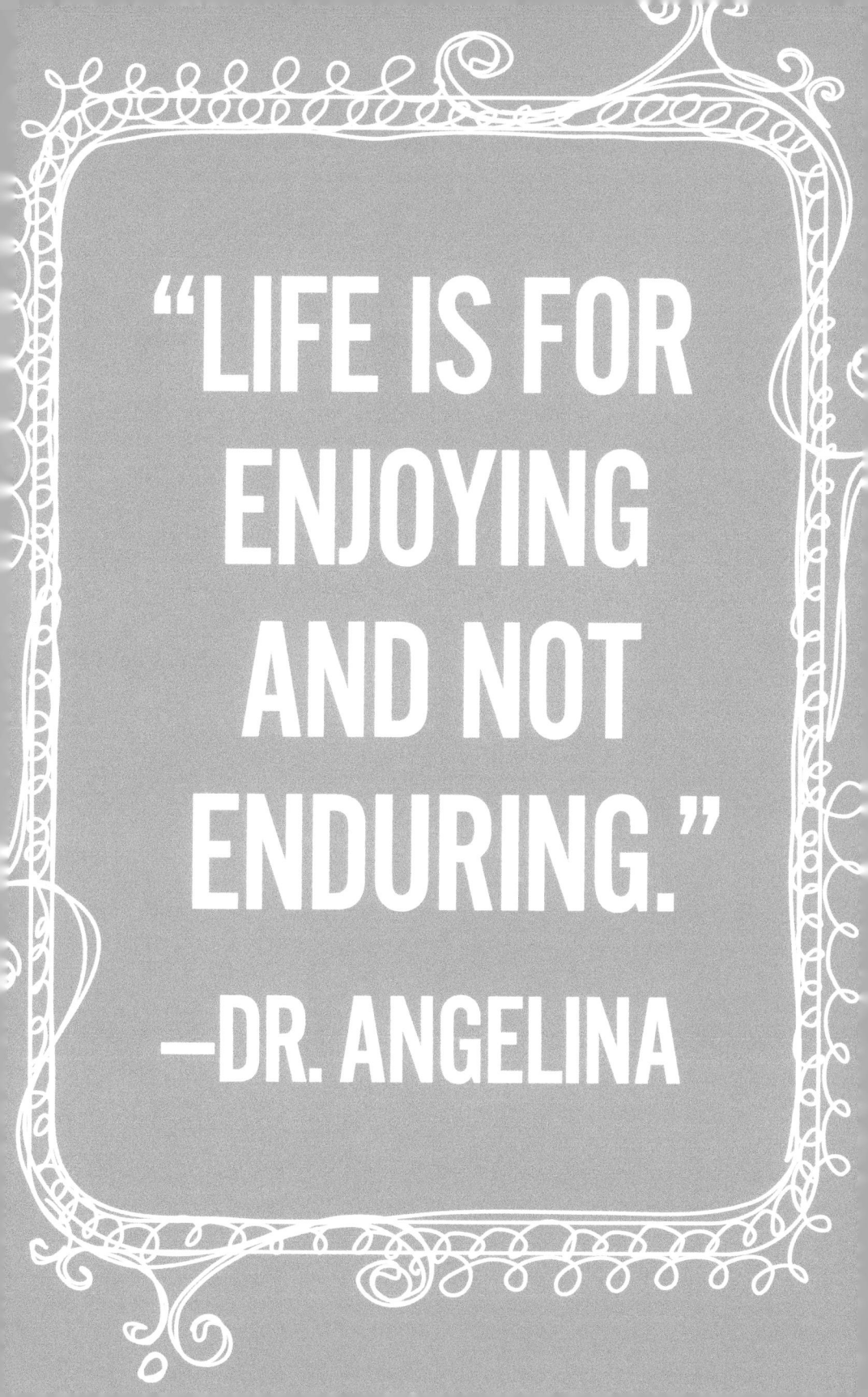

TRUE HAPPINESS DOESN'T HAPPEN OVERNIGHT.

APPENDIX
BLOCKING THE NOISE: QUICK TIPS AND CHEAT SHEETS

ACCEPTANCE MANTRAS

- "Let go and let God."
- "I will have the courage to experience the beauty of life."
- "It's not that deep."
- "Think before you speak."
- "True happiness doesn't happen overnight."

DETACHMENT MANTRAS

- "I will love you for who you are, but I won't be connected to your noise."
- "I didn't cause it, I can't control it, and I can't cure it."
- "I accept you for who you are and will no longer attempt to change you."
- "Detachment is not rejection; it is love for myself and appreciation for those I love."
- "E (expectation), P (preparation), A (accommodation) before I begin each day."

THE CHAIN OF GRATITUDE

ACCEPT that you cannot change another person >> Feel **EMPATHY** for the person engaging in noisy behavior >> Focus on the **GRATITUDE** you have for that person and their role in your life

> **Quick tips:**
>
> *The next time you're about to panic, take a deep breath and ask yourself: "How will I feel about that a week from now?" More likely than not, whatever you're panicking about is so insignificant in the grand scheme of life that you'll never think about it again—so why let it derail your day?*
>
> *Remember the phrase "Observe, not absorb." We can appreciate the people around us without internalizing their noise.*
>
> *When you're unsure whether a thought is noise or a fact, ask yourself: "Would I say this to a trusted friend?" If the answer is no, you can toss that thought in the noise bin and move on with your day.*

NOISY THOUGHTS: A CHEAT SHEET

While noisy thoughts can feel very specific and personal, most cognitive distortions belong to one of ten categories. Being able to categorize your noisy thoughts is like following your clothing's care instructions on laundry day: you can toss them all into the washer in one massive heap, but you'll get better results if you separate them and care for them according to specific instructions.

All-or-nothing thinking: These are thoughts that color your world in absolutes. Rather than a world of possibilities, you see two opposite extremes with no in-between.

Overgeneralization: This is when one flaw, failure, mistake, or negative experience becomes how you define yourself or an aspect of your life—for example, believing that a failed relationship means you're unworthy of love or meant to be alone forever.

Mental filtering: This is the tendency to ignore the positive and see only the negative.

Jumping to conclusions: This is the inaccurate belief that you know how a situation will end or what another person is thinking. It often involves assuming the worst, regardless of the facts.

Magnification and minimization: This is the tendency to emphasize or focus on the negatives, while diminishing the importance or likelihood of the positives.

Emotional reasoning: This is when you give your feelings the status of fact, without accounting for the transient nature of emotions or any other factors beyond your present emotional state.

"Should" statements: This is when your thoughts are clouded with critical judgments that center on the words "should," "shouldn't," "must," "ought to," and "have to."

Labeling: This happens when you assign an overgeneralized label to yourself or others, based on one negative experience.

Fallacy of change: These thoughts come in two forms: external and internal. When they're external, you believe you have the ability to change someone else's feelings or behaviors. When they're internal, you believe that your life is beyond your control and there's nothing you can do to change it.

Personalization: This happens when you feel compelled to take responsibility for situations or issues that have nothing to do with you. You take the blame for events that are out of your control and impossible for you to influence.

ABOUT THE AUTHOR

Dr. Angelina Lipman has distinguished herself as a psychologist, educator, author, and founder of Blocking the Noise. As an accomplished writer and researcher, she has contributed widely cited pieces to the *Annual Review of Psychology,* the *Journal of Personality and Social Psychology,* and *Social Justice Research.*

Dr. Angelina received her Bachelor of Arts in Psychology from Columbia University, a Master's degree in Psychology from New York University, and a PhD in Social Personality Psychology from New York University. Dr. Angelina spent over a decade in academia, with a research focus on the impact of identity on psychological well-being, achievement, and relationships. Her work has been recognized via numerous awards, fellowships, and conferences.

Dr. Angelina is passionate about creating a platform for accessible wellness. Blocking the Noise is the culmination of her commitment to empower anyone, anywhere, at any time to remove negativity and experience unwavering happiness.

Dr. Angelina resides in Westchester, New York, with her husband, three children, and many pets.

ACKNOWLEDGMENTS

I ascribe to the philosophy it takes a village to raise a child. As I began the journey of blocking the noise, I quickly learned that these simple words of wisdom are not limited to parenthood. It took a village to make this book.

First and foremost, I have to acknowledge my extraordinary family, who were the inspiration for creating the blocking the noise program. Their love, wisdom, and support were integral to the process.

My husband, Monte, is the epitome of blocking the noise. He has been my sounding board, discerning critic, and champion throughout the many years it took to finish this book. I am forever grateful and could not have done this without his steadfast belief in my vision for blocking the noise.

My desire to create the Blocking the Noise program stems from my children. Being their mother is the greatest gift. While there are hills and valleys to being a mother, I am grateful for each day. My greatest accomplishment in life is being Remy, Juliet, and Cameron's mother. In some sense, this book is a love letter to my children. I always want them to remember that life is for the living. I hope that this book will be a constant reminder to enjoy and never endure life.

As you age, it is often easy to forget about the pivotal role our parents and grandparents play. I want to acknowledge my parents' as well as grandparents' impact on shaping the person I am today. I am grateful for their lessons on the importance of hard work, perseverance, and following your dreams. My father taught me the importance of being a good listener and the art of storytelling. My mother bestowed a steadfast faith that has been a source of great comfort throughout my life. My grandparents exemplified the importance of being an active community member and taking the time to encourage and help others.

I would like to thank my Auntie Pattie for her love and kindness throughout my life. She taught me the true meaning of gratitude.

I would be remiss to not acknowledge the talented editors and designers who helped ensure the efficacy of this book. Thank you Rick Florino,

Stephanie Georgopulos, Will Palmer, and Catherine Casalino for sharing your amazing gifts with me. Rick, thank you for your encouragement and unwavering support. Stephanie, thank you for your sense of humor and critical eye. Will, thank you for your keen sense of structure and grammar. Catherine, thank you for making my vision come to life in ways I could only imagine. Each of you has helped me become a stronger writer, teacher, and student. Undoubtedly, the Blocking the Noise program is better because of your dedication and commitment.

Thank you to my mentors Geraldine Downey, Niall Bolger, and Tom Tyler. I am grateful for your guidance and showing me the importance of research. You instilled a passion for social impact and the ability to make data actionable.

I would like to acknowledge my A-Team. Friends and family whose love, support, guidance, and presence are the cornerstones of how I block the noise each and every day. I am humbled by your unconditional love. I would like to give a special thank you to my cousin and best friend Therese. I am truly grateful for your friendship.

Last but certainly not least, I would like to thank the reader. Thank you for being an integral part of blocking the noise.

JOURNAL PAGES

Notes...

JOURNAL PAGES • 151

Notes...

Notes...

Notes...

Notes...

LIFE IS FOR THE LIVING